# Studies In Tape Reading

By
Rollo
Tape

The Ticker Publishing Company, New York

# Contents.

# Studies in Tape Reading

## I.  Introductory

THERE is a widespread demand for more light on the subject of Tape Reading. Thousands of traders entertain the idea that in some way the market momentarily indicates its own immediate future; that these indications are accurately recorded on the tape; therefore he who can interpret what is imprinted on the narrow paper ribbon has within his reach unlimited wealth.

It seems to me that such an opinion is fully warranted for *it is well known that many of the most successful traders and operators of the present day began operations by successful Tape Reading, trading in fractional lots of stock with a capital of only a few hundred dollars.*

Success of
Tape Readers

Speaking of Joe Manning, one of the shrewdest and most successful of all the traders on the floor of the New York Stock Exchange, a friend of mine once said:

**Joe Manning**

"Joe and I used to trade in ten share lots together. He was an ordinary trader, just as I am. We used to hang over the same ticker."

The speaker was, at the time he made the remark, still trading in ten-share lots, while I happened to know that Joe's bank balance—his active working capital—amounted to $100,000, and that this represents but a part of the fortune built on his ability to interpret the language of the tape.

*Why* was one of these men able to amass a fortune, while the other never acquired more than a few thousand dollars at the same pursuit? Their chances were equal at the start so far as capital and opportunity go. The millions were there waiting to be won by either or both.

**Mental Qualifications**

The answer seems to be in the peculiar mental qualifications, highly potent in the successful trader, but unpossessed by the other. There is, of course, a small element of luck in every case, but pure luck could not be so sustained in Manning's case as to carry him through operations covering a term of years.

By proper mental equipment we do not mean the mere ability to take a loss, define the trend, or to execute some other move characteristic of the professional trader. We refer to the active or dormant qualities in his make-up. The power to drill himself into the right mental attitude; to stifle his emotion, fear, anxiety, elation, recklessness, to train his mind into obedience so that it recognizes but one master—the tape—these, if possessed, would be as valuable in shaping the result as natural ability, or what is called the sixth sense in trading.

Some people are born musicians, others seemingly void of musical taste, *develop* themselves into virtuosos. It is the amount of I WILL in a man which makes him mediocre or pre-eminent—in Wall Street parlance, a dub or a big trader.

**Jacob Field**

Jacob Field is another exponent of Tape Reading. Those who knew "Jakey" when he began his Wall Street career, were impressed by his ability to read the tape, and follow the trend. His talent for this work was doubtless born in him; time and experience have intensified it until now he is considered by the majority of his fellows, the Prince of Floor Traders.

**Jim Keene**

Whatever laurels Mr. Keene has won as an operator or syndicate manager, do not detract from his reputation as a Tape Reader. His scrutiny of the tape is so intense that he appears to be in a trance while his mental processes are being worked out. He seems to analyze prices, volumes and fluctuations down to the finest imaginable point, then telephones to the floor to ascertain the character of the buying or selling in certain active stocks. With this auxiliary information he completes his judgment and makes his commitments.

Mr. Keene stands to-day on the pinnacle of fame as a Tape Reader, and his daily presence at the ticker is sufficient evidence that the work pays and pays well.

One might say: "These are rare examples. The average man never makes a success of Tape Reading."

Right you are! The *average* man seldom makes a success of anything.

Success in this field usually results from years of painstaking effort and absolute concentration upon the subject. It requires that one devote his whole time and attention to the tape. He should have no other business or profession.

"A man cannot serve two masters," and the tape is a tyrant.

**Study Necessary**

One cannot become a Tape Reader by giving the ticker absent treatment; nor by running into his broker's office after lunch, or seeing "how the market closed" from his evening newspaper. He cannot study this art from the far end of a telegraph or telephone wire. He should spend twenty-seven hours a week at the ticker, and many more hours away from it studying his mistakes and finding the "why" of his losses.

If Tape Reading were an exact science, one would simply have to assemble the factors, carry out the operations indicated, and trade accordingly. But the factors influencing the market are infinite in their number and character, as well as in their effect upon the market, and to attempt the construction of a Tape Reading formula would seem to be futile. However, something of the kind (in the rough) may develop as we progress in this investigation, so let us preserve open minds.

What is Tape Reading?

This question may be best answered by first deciding what it is not.

Tape Reading is not merely looking at the tape to ascertain how prices are running.

**What Tape Reading is Not**

It is not reading the news and then buying or selling "if the stock acts right."

It is not trading on tips, opinions, or information.

It is not buying "because they are going up," or selling "because they look weak."

It is not trading on chart indications or by other mechanical methods.

It is not "buying on dips and selling on bulges."

Nor is it any of the hundred other foolish things practised by the millions of people without method, forethought or calculation.

Tape Reading seems to us: The science of determining from the tape the immediate trend of prices.

**Tape Reading Defined**

It is judging from what appears on

the tape *now,* what is likely to be shown in five minutes or more.

It bears no relation to clairvoyancy and we do not believe that spirits of departed friends could be of assistance to students.

Tape Reading is rapid-fire horse sense. Its object is to determine whether Union Pacific, which is now 159, will sell at 160 before 158, or vice versa; to make deductions from each succeeding transaction—every shift of the market kaleidoscope; to grasp a new situation, force it lightning-like through the weighing machine of the brain, and to reach a decision which can be acted upon with coolness and precision—all within the space of a few seconds.

**Supply and Demand**

It is gauging the momentary supply and demand in particular stocks and in the whole market, comparing the forces behind each and their relationship, each to the other and to all.

A Tape Reader is like the manager of a department store; into his office are poured hundreds of reports of sales made by the various departments. He notes the general trend of business— whether demand is heavy or light throughout the store—but lends special attention to the lines in which demand is abnormally strong or weak. When he finds difficulty in keeping his shelves full in a certain department, he instructs his buyers, and they increase their buying orders; when certain goods do not move he knows there is little demand (market) for them, therefore, he lowers his prices —offers inducements to possible purchasers.

A floor trader who stands in one crowd all day is like the buyer for one department—he sees more quickly than anyone else the demand for that class of goods, but has no way of comparing it to that prevailing in other parts of the store.

He may be trading on the long side of Union Pacific, which has a strong upward trend, when suddenly a break in another stock will demoralize the market in Union Pacific, and he will be forced to compete with others who have stocks to sell.

The Tape Reader, on the other hand, from his perch at the ticker, enjoys a bird's eye view of the whole field. When serious weakness develops in any quarter, he is quick to note, weigh and act.

**Advantages of the Tape Reader**

Another advantage in favor of the Tape Reader: The tape tells the news minutes, hours and days before the news tickers, or newspapers, and before it can become current gossip. Everything from a foreign war to the passing of a dividend; from a Supreme Court decision to the ravages of the boll weevil is reflected primarily upon the tape.

The insider who knows a dividend is to be jumped from 6 per cent. to 10 per cent. shows his hand on the tape when he attempts to turn his knowledge into dollars, and the investor with 100 shares to sell makes his fractional impress upon its market price.

The market is like a slowly revolving wheel. Whether the wheel will continue to revolve in the same direction, stand still or reverse depends entirely upon the forces which come in contact with its hub and tread. Even when the contact is broken, and nothing remains to affect its course, the wheel retains a certain impulse from the most recent dominating force, and revolves until it comes to a standstill or is subjected to other influences.

The engineers who harnessed Niagara had a simple task compared to that of the Tape Reader. The cataract which he undertakes to control seemingly has cross-currents and maelstroms, reversing its direction and defying the laws of gravity. To divert a portion of this unruly Wall Street stream, to subject it to his will, seems like a task for a superman. Yet it can be done, for others have done it.

**Manipulation**

The element of manipulation need not discourage any one. Manipulators are giant traders, wearing seven-leagued boots. The trained ear can detect the steady "clump, clump," as they progress, and the footprints are recognized in enormous quantities of stock appearing on the tape. Little fellows are at liberty to tiptoe wherever the footprints lead, but they must be wary that the giants do not turn quickly and crush them.

## Introductory

The Tape Reader has many advantages over the long swing operator. He never ventures far from shore; that is, he plays with a close stop, never laying himself open to a large loss. Accidents or catastrophes cannot seriously injure him because he can reverse his position in an instant, and follow the new-formed stream from source to mouth. As his position on either the long or short side is confirmed and emphasized, he increases his line, thus following up and cumulating the advantage gained.

A Secure Position

A simon-pure Tape Reader does not care to carry stocks over night. The tape is then silent, and he only knows what to do when it tells him. Something may occur at midnight which may crumple up his diagram of the next day's market. He leaves nothing to chance; hence he prefers a clean sheet when the 3 o'clock gong strikes.

By this method interest charges are avoided, reducing the percentage against him to a considerable extent.

The Tape Reader is like a vendor of fruit who, each morning, provides himself with a stock of the choicest and mose seasonable products, and for which there is the greatest demand. He pays his cash and disposes of the goods as quickly as possible, at a profit varying from 50 to 100 per cent. on cost. To carry his stock over night causes a loss on account of spoilage. This corresponds with the interest charge to the trader.

The fruit vendor is successful because he knows what and when to buy, also where and how to sell. But there are stormy days when he cannot go out; when buyers do not appear; when he is arrested, fined, or locked up by a blue-coated despot or his wares are scattered abroad by a careless truckman.

Wall Street will readily apply these situations to the various attitudes in which the Tape Reader finds himself.

**Periods of Loss**

He ventures $100 to make $200, and as the market goes in his favor his risk is reduced, but there are times when he finds himself at sea, with his stock deteriorating. Or the market is so unsettled that he does not know how to act; he is caught on stop or held motionless in a dead market; he takes a series of losses, or is obliged to be away from the tape when opportunities occur. His calculations are completely upset by some unforeseen event or his capital is impaired by overtrading or poor judgment.

The vendor does not hope to buy a barrel of apples for $3 and sell them the same day for $300. He expects to make from nothing to $3 a day. He depends upon a small but certain profit, which will average enough over a week or a month to pay him for his time and labor.

This is the objective point of the Tape Reader—to make an average profit. In a month's operations he may make $3,500 and lose $3,000—a net profit of $500 to show for his work. If he can keep this average up, trading in 100-share lots, throughout a year, he has only to increase his unit to 200, 300, and 500 shares or more, and the results will be tremendous.

The amount of capital or the size of the order is of secondary importance to this question: Can you trade in and out of all kinds of markets and show an average profit of say ⅛ per cent. per day? If so, you are proficient in the art. If you can trade with only a small average loss per day, or come out even, you are rapidly getting there.

**Average Profits**

In the December TICKER there was set forth the record made by a trader whose operations showed 42 profits out of 71 trades, the gross points profit being 50⅜ against 37¼ gross points loss. This was good work, although the commissions and tax threw the net result over into a loss of 6 points. We mention this merely to show the standard by which success in Tape Reading should be measured.

The trader who there disclosed the outcome of his efforts was not a Tape Reader. He operated largely upon information and had no fixed method.

A Tape Reader abhors information and follows a definite and thoroughly tested plan, which after months and years of practice becomes second nature to him. His mind forms habits which operate automatically in guiding his market ventures.

No intelligent human need be told that

when the sky darkens and the thunder rolls there's likely to be a shower. He unconsciously notes the preliminary signs, dons a raincoat and takes an umbrella.

Long practice will make the Tape Reader just as proficient in forecasting stock market events, but his intuition will be reinforced by logic, reason and analysis.

**The Scalper**

Here we find the characteristics which distinguish the Tape Reader from the Scalper. The latter is essentially one who tries to grab a point or two profit "without rhyme or reason"—he don't care how, so long as he gets it.

A Scalper will trade on a tip, a look, a guess, a hearsay, on what he thinks or what a friend of a friend of Morgan's says.

The Tape Reader evolves himself into an automaton which takes note of a situation, weighs it, decides upon a course and gives an order. There is no quickening of the pulse, no nerves, no hopes or fears. The result produces neither elation nor depression. There is equanimity before, during and after the trade.

The Scalper is a bob-tailed car with rattling windows, a jouncing motion and a strong tendency to jump the track.

The Tape Reader is like a Pullman coach, which travels smoothly and steadily along the roadbed of the tape, acquiring direction and speed from the market engine, and being influenced by nothing else whatever.

Having thus described our ideal Tape Reader in a general way, let us inquire into some of the requisite qualifications.

First, he must be absolutely self-reliant. A dependent person whose judgment hangs upon that of others will find himself swayed by a thousand outside influences. At critical points his judgment will be useless. He must be able to say: "The facts are—; the resulting indications are—; therefore I will do thus and so."

Next he must be familiar with the technicalities of the market, so that every little incident affecting prices will be given due weight. He should know the history, earnings and financial condition of the companies in whose stock he is trading; the ways of the manipulators; the different kinds of markets; be able to measure the effect of news and rumors; know when and in what stocks it is best to trade; measure the forces behind them; know when to cut a loss and take a profit.

He must study the various swings and know where the market and his particular stock stand; must recognize the inherent weakness or strength of the market; understand the basis or logic of movements. He should study the fundamentals and sift the wheat from the chaff; recognize the turning points of the market; see in his mind's eye what is happening on the floor.

**Nerve and Patience**

He must have the nerve to stand a series of losses; persistence to keep him at the work during adverse periods; self-control to avoid overtrading and a phlegmatic disposition to ballast and balance him at all times.

For perfect concentration as a protection from the tips, gossip and other influences which abound in a broker's office, he should, if possible, seclude himself. A tiny room with a ticker, a desk and private telephone connection with his broker's office are all the facilities required. The work requires such delicate balance of the faculties that the slightest influence either way may throw the result against the trader. He may say: "Nothing influences me," but unconsciously it does affect his judgment to know that another man is bearish at a point where he thinks stocks should be bought. The mere thought, "He may be right," has a deterring influence upon him; he hesitates; the opportunity is lost. No matter how the market goes from that point, he has missed a cog and his mental machinery is thrown out of gear. Silence is a much needed lubricant to the Tape Reader's mind.

**Seclusion**

The advisability of having even a news ticker in the room, is a subject for discussion.

The tape tells the present and future of the market.

## Introductory

The news ticker records what *has* happened. It announces the cause for the effect which has already been more or less felt in the market.

Money is made in Tape Reading by anticipating what is coming—not by waiting till it happens and going with the crowd.

**News**

The *effect* of news is an entirely different proposition. Considerable light is thrown on the technical strength or weakness of the market and special stocks by their action in the face of important news. For the moment it seems to us that a news ticker might be admitted to the sanctum, provided its whisperings are given only the weight to which they are entitled.

To evolve a practical method—one which *any* trader may use in his daily operations and which those with varying proficiency in the art of Tape Reading will find of value and assistance—such is the task we have set before us in this series. Perhaps we shall succeed; perhaps not.

**Our Task**

We will consider all the market factors of vital importance in Tape Reading, as well as methods used by experts. These will be illustrated by reproductions from the tape. Every effort will be made to produce something of definite, tangible value to those who are now operating in a hit-or-miss sort of way.

## II.  Preliminary Suggestions

Actual
Trading
Necessary

WHEN embarking on any new enterprise, the first thing to consider is the amount of capital required.  To study Tape Reading "on paper" is one thing, but to practice and become proficient in the art is quite another.  Almost anyone can make money on imaginary trades, for these require no risk of any kind— the mind is free from the strain which accompanies an actual venture; fear does not enter into the situation; patience is unlimited.

All this is changed when even a small market commitment is made.  The trader of slight experience suffers mental anguish if the stock does not instantly go his way; he is afraid of a large loss, hence his judgment becomes warped, and he closes the trade in order to secure mental relief.

As these are all symptoms of inexperience, they cannot be overcome by avoiding the issue.  The brave and the business-like thing to do is to wade right into the game and learn to play it under conditions which are to be met and conquered before success can be attained.

After a complete absorption of every available piece of educational writing bearing upon Tape Reading, it is best to commence trading in ten share lots, so as to acquire genuine trading experience. This may not suit some people with a propensity for gambling, and who look upon the ten-share trader as a piker. The average lamb with $10,000 **Start Small** wants to commence with 100 to 500-share lots—he wishes to start at the top and work down. It is only a question of time when he will have to trade in ten-share lots.

To us it seems better to start at the bottom with ten shares. There is plenty of time in which to increase the unit if you are successful. If success is not eventually realized you will be many dollars better off for having ventured the minimum quantity.

It has already been shown in THE TICKER'S Inquiry Column that the market for odd lots on the New York Stock Exchange is most satisfactory, so there is no other excuse for the novice who desires to trade in round lots than greed-of-gain, or get-rich-quick. Think of a baby, just learning to walk, being entered in a race with professional sprinters!

In the previous chapter we suggested that success in Tape Reading should be measured by the number of *points* profit over *points* lost. For all practical purposes, therefore, we might trade in one-share lots, were there no objection on the part of our broker, and if this quantity were not so absurdly small as to invite careless executions. Ten shares is really the smallest quantity that should be considered, but we mention one share simply to impress upon our readers that in studying Tape Reading, better keep in mind that you are playing for *points,* not dollars. The dollars will come along fast enough if you can make more points *net* than you lose. The professional billiardist playing for a stake aims to *out-point* his antagonist. After trading for a few months do not consider the dollars you are ahead or behind, but analyze the record in points. In this way your progress may be studied.

**Points, Not Dollars**

As the initial losses in trading are likely to be heavy, and as the estimated capital must be a more or less arbitrary amount, we should say that units of $1,000 would be necessary for each ten-share lot traded in at the beginning. This allows for 90 points more losses than profits, and still leaves margin with which to proceed. Some people will secure a footing with less capital; others may be obliged to put up several units of $1,000 each before they begin to show profits; still others will spend a fortune (large or small) without making

**Capital**

it pay, or meeting with any encouragement.

Look over R. G. Dun & Co.'s Causes of Commercial Failures, as recently tabulated in this magazine, and you will find the chief causes to be: (1) Lack of capital, and (2) Incompetence.

Lack of capital in Wall Street operations can usually be traced to over-trading. This bears out the epigram "Over-trading is financial suicide." It may mean too large a quantity of stock in the initial operations, or if the trader loses money, he may not reduce the size of his trade to correspond with the shrinkage in his capital.

To make our point clear: A man starts trading in 100-share lots on 20 points margin. After a series of losses he finds that he has only $200 remaining. This is still 20 points on ten shares, but does he reduce his orders? No. He risks the $200 on a 50 or 100-share trade in a last desperate effort to recoup. After being wiped out he tells his friends how he "could have made money if he had had more capital."

Incompetence really deserves first place in the list. Supreme ignorance is the predominant feature of both Wall Street lamb and seasoned speculator. It is surprising how many people stay in the Street year after year, acquiring nothing more, apparently, than a keen scent for tips and gossip. Ask them a technical question that smacks of scientific knowledge of the tape, and they are unable to reply.

Such folks are there for one of two reasons: They have either been "lucky" or their margins are replenished from some source outside of Wall Street.

The proportion of commercial failures due to Lack of Capital or Incompetence is about 60 per cent. Call the former by its Wall Street cognomen—Overtrading—and the percentage of stock market disasters traceable thereto would be about 90.

Success is only for the few, and the problem is to ascertain, with the minimum expenditure of time and money, whether you are fitted for the work.

These, in a nutshell, are the vital questions up to this point:

Have you technical knowledge of the market and the factors which move it?

Have you $1,000 or more which you can afford to lose in an effort to demonstrate your ability at Tape Reading?

Can you devote your entire time and attention to the study and the practice of this science?

Are you so fixed financially that you are not dependent upon your possible profits, and so that you will not suffer if none are forthcoming now or later?

## Preliminary Suggestions

There is no sense in mincing words over this matter, nor in holding out false encouragement to people who are looking for an easy, drop-a-penny-in-the-slot way of making money. Tape Reading is hard work, hence those who are mentally lazy need not apply.

Nor should anyone to whom it will mean worry as to where his bread and butter is coming from. Money-worry is not conducive to clear-headedness. Over-anxiety upsets the equilibrium of a trader more than anything else. So if you cannot afford the time and money, and have not the necessary supply of patience, better wait. Start right or not at all.

**Choice of Brokers**

Having decided to proceed, the trader who is equal to the foregoing circumstances finds himself asking, "Where shall I trade?"

The choice of a broker is an important matter to the Tape Reader. He should find one especially equipped for the work: who can give close attention to his orders, furnish quick bid and asked prices, and other technical information, such as the quantities wanted and offered at different levels, etc. The broker most to be desired should never have so much business on hand that he cannot furnish the trader with a verbal flashlight of what the crowd in this or that stock is doing, at any particular moment. This is important, for at times it will be money in the pocket to know just in what momentary position one stock or the market stands. The broker who is not over-burdened with business can give this service; he can also devote time and care to the execution of orders.

Let me give an instance of how this works out in practice: You are long 100 Union, with a stop-order just under the market price; a dip comes and 100 shares sells at your stop price—say 164. Your careful, and not too busy broker stands in the crowd. He observes that several thousand shares are bid for at 164 and only a few hundred offered at the price. He does not sell the stock, but waits to see if it won't rally. It does rally. You are given a new lease of life. This handling of the order may benefit you $50, $100 or several hundred dollars in each instance, and is an advantage to be sought when choosing a broker.

**Handling an Order**

The house which transacts an active commission business for a large clientele is unable to give this service. Its stop-orders and other orders not "close to the market," must be given to Specialists, and the press of business is such that it cannot devote especial attention to the orders of any one client. Hence, it would seem that our Tape Reader had better search for a small commission house which has one New York Stock Exchange member, an office partner and only one or two employees.

## Preliminary Suggestions

The number of clerks is a good index to the amount of business done. Their fewness is not a reflection on the strength, standing, or brokerage ability of the house. Some people are good brokers and have ample capital, but they do not understand the science of business getting.

Small House Best

In a small house, such as we have described, the Tape Reader is less likely to be bothered by a gallery of traders, with their diverse and loud-spoken opinions. In other words, he will be left more or less to himself and be free to concentrate upon his task.

The ticker should be within calling distance of the telephone to the Stock Exchange. Some brokers have a way of making you or a clerk walk a mile to give an order. Every step means delay. The elapse of a few seconds may result in a lost market or opportunity. If you are in a small private room away from the order desk, there should be a special telephone connecting you with the order clerk. Ponderous, ice-wagon methods won't go in Tape Reading.

Orders should generally be given "at the market." We make this statement as a result of long experience and observation, and believe we can demonstrate the advisability of it.

The process of reporting transactions on the tape, as recently set forth in these pages, consumes from five seconds to say five minutes, depending upon the activity of the market. For argument's sake, let us consider that the *average* interval between the time a sale takes place on the floor and the report appears on the tape is half a minute.

**Giving Orders**  A market order in an active stock is usually executed and reported to the customer in about two minutes. Half this time is consumed in putting your broker into the crowd with the order in hand; the other half in writing out and transmitting the report. Hence, when Union Pacific comes 164 on the tape and you instantly decide to buy it, the period of time between your decision and the execution of your order is as follows:

Minutes.

The tape is behind the market . . ½
Time elapsed before broker can execute the order ................1

1½

It will therefore be seen that your decision is based on a price which prevailed half a minute ago, and that you must purchase if you will, at the price at which the stock stands one minute hence. This might happen between your decision and the execution of your order:

UP 164. ⅛. ¼. ⅜. ½. ¼. ⅛. 164,

and yours might be the last hundred. When the report arrived you could not swear that it was bought at 164 before or after it touched 164½. Or you

—28—

might get it at 164½, even though it was 164 when you gave the order, and when the report was handed to you.

Just as often the opposite will take place—the stock will go in your favor. In fact, the thing averages up in the long run, so that traders who do not give market orders are hurting their own chances.

An infinite number of traders, seeing Union Pacific at 164, will say: **Limited Orders**

"Buy me a hundred at 164."

The broker who is not too busy will go into the crowd, and, finding the stock at 164⅛@¼ will report back to the office that "Union is ⅛ bid."

The trader gives his broker no credit for this service; instead, he considers it a sign that his broker, the floor traders and the insiders have all conspired to make him pay ¼ per cent. higher for his 100 shares, so he replies:

"Let it stand at 164. If they don't give it to me at that, I won't buy it at all."

How foolish! Yet characteristic of the style of reasoning used by the public. His argument is that the stock, for good and sufficient reasons, is a splendid purchase at 164. At 164⅛ or ¼ these reasons are completely nullified; the stock becomes dear, or he cares more to foil the plans of this "band of robbers" than for a possible profit.

If a stock is cheap at 164 it's cheap at 164¼.

If you can't trust your broker, get another.

If you think the law of supply and demand is altered to catch your $25, better reorganize your thinkery.

**On the Floor**

Were you on the floor you could probably buy at 164 the minute it touched that figure, but of this there is no certainty. You would, however, be 1½ minutes nearer to the market. Your commission charges would also be practically eliminated. Therefore, if you have seventy or eighty thousand dollars lying around the house which you do not especially need, buy a seat. If you have not, cease the uproar.

A Tape Reader who deserves the name, makes money in spite of commissions, taxes and delays.

**Arthur Livermore**

Arthur Livermore used to trade solely on what the tape told him, closing out everything before three o'clock. He traded from an office and paid the regular commissions, yet three trades out of five showed profits. Having made a fortune, he invested it in bonds and gave them all to his wife. Anticipating the 1907 panic, he put his $13,000 automobile up for a loan of $5,000, and with this capital started to play the bear side, using his profits as additional margin. At one time he was short 70,000 shares of Union Pacific. His whole line was covered on one of the panic days, and his net profits were a million dollars!

To return to the question of giving orders: Anyone who says, "This stock should be bought but I will not pay ⅛ above my price for it," is like a man who thinks he can make certain money if he could but get to Chicago. Arriving at the ticket office he finds that the fare is $2 more than he expected, but though well heeled, he refuses to pay the required amount and abandons the trip.

**Get on Board!**

If you don't get aboard your train, you'll never arrive.

Giving limited orders loses more good dollars than it saves. We refer, of course, to orders in the big, active stocks, wherein the bid and asked prices are usually ⅛ apart. Especially is this true in closing out a trade. Many foolish people are interminably hung up because they try to save eighths by giving limited orders in a market that is running away from them.

For the Tape Reader there is a psychological moment when he must open or close his trade. His orders must therefore be "at the market." Haggling over fractions will make him lose the thread of the tape, upset his poise and interrupt the workings of his mental machinery.

In scale buying or selling it is obvious that limited orders must be used. There are certain other times when they are of advantage, but as the Tape

**Scale Trading**

Reader generally goes with the trend it is a case of "get on or get left."

By all means "get on."

This is an important matter, and should be decided in a general way before one starts to trade. Let's nose around a little and see what we can reason out.

If you are trading in 100-share lots, your stock must move your way one point to make $100 profit.

Which class of stocks are most likely to move a point? Answer: The high-priced issues.

Looking over the records we find that a stock selling around 150 will average 2½ points fluctuation a day, while one selling at 50 will average only one point. Consequently, you have 2½ times more action in the higher priced stock.

The commission and tax charges are the same in both. Interest charges are three times as large, but this is an insignificant item to the Tape Reader who closes out his trades each day.

The higher priced stocks also cover a greater number of points during the year or cycle than those of lower price —Union Pacific from 195⅜ down to par (95⅜ points), against Steel common from 50⅜ down to 21⅞ (28½ points) being recent striking examples. Stocks like Great Northern, although enjoying a much wider range, are not desirable for trading purposes when up to 300 or more—fluctuations and bid and

asked prices are too far apart to per-
mit rapid in-and-out trading.

The trend of the general market is
largely made by the following stocks,
in the order named:

Union Pacific
Reading
Steel Common
St. Paul
Amalgamated
Smelters

Union Pacific is the leader because it
is the pivotal stock of the Harriman
group, there is a large floating supply,
a broad market and wide swings; it is
popular with floor traders, big and little.
Southern Pacific is its running mate, but
owing to the smaller number of shares
of the latter afloat, it seldom dis-
putes for the leadership. The speculative
possibilities in Union Pacific are so
enormous, and the methods of Harriman and his associates so calculated to
keep the public on tip-toe that the stock
responds instantly to every wave of sentiment.

Reading from the top to the bottom
of the last swing (164 to 70½) made
94½ points, practically the same as
Union Pacific. Its daily swings also
about correspond. There is only $70,-
000,000 of it outstanding. The floating
supply is small, owing to the large blocks
that are held by other roads, or by permanent investors. Hence, it is easy to
manipulate. The comparative scarcity

—33—

of the stock is shown in the frequency of ¼ point fluctuations between sales.

It is a very satisfactory stock for Tape Reading operations.

**U. S. Steel**

Steel common is lumbering in its movements, thus reflecting the five million shares outstanding and the consequent widespread public interest. It is useful as a barometer of the market and of public sentiment, but its swings. are rarely wide enough for the Tape Reader, as they average only about a point a day.

**St. Paul**

St. Paul is one of the truest stocks for trading purposes. It is manipulated at times, but generally it responds automatically to the slightest change in market temper. Its daily movements are wide, about equal to Union Pacific and Reading. Its last big swing was 106 points.

**Amalgamated Copper**

Amalgamated is at present only a secondary leader, and taking the year through not nearly as satisfactory to deal in as some of the others above mentioned. Its swing in 1907 was about 80 points.

**Smelters**

Smelters is one of the most highly manipulated issues on the list, erratic, often difficult to follow, at other times easy. Its daily range is usually equal to any of the others, and its last big swing was about 116 points. One gets plenty of action in Smelters, but not nearly the steadiness, nor the clearly de-

fined trend prevailing in the big railroads.

As a result of observation and years
of trading experience, we prefer Union
Pacific to any other, because of the
qualities to which we have referred.  In
its present range (between 160 and 170)
it is below the price warranted by its
dividend rate and equities.  This makes
it especially responsive to bullish news
and better adapted for trading on the
long side.

Best Stocks
for the Tape
Reader

If obliged to choose a second stock,
Reading would appeal to us as offering
the next greatest advantages.  While
Reading contains enormous intrinsic
value it is at present a 4 per cent. stock
selling in the 130s—a price scarcely warranted if its rate were increased to 5
per cent.  So, for the time being at least,
Reading affords the best medium for
short selling.

These two issues are the chief hinges
on which the door of the market turns
—Union the upper, Reading the lower
hinge.  It is unnecessary for anyone to
go beyond these except in times when
the industrials dominate the market; in
this case, Amalgamated, Smelters or
Steel will replace them temporarily.

It is better for a Tape Reader to trade
in one stock than two or more.  Stocks
have habits and characteristics which
are as distinct as those of human beings
or animals.  By a close study the trader
becomes intimately acquainted with

Trade in
One Stock
at a Time

these habits and is able to anticipate the stock's action under given circumstances. A stock may be stubborn, sensitive, irresponsive, complaisant, aggressive; it may dominate the tape or trail along behind the rest; it is whimsical and coquettish; it may whisper, babble like a brook or roar like a cataract. Its moods must be studied if you would know it and bend it to your will.

Study implies concentration. A person who trades in a dozen stocks at a time cannot concentrate on one.

The popular method of trading (which means the unsuccessful way) is to say:

"I think the market's a sale. Smelters, Copper and St. Paul have had the biggest rise lately; they ought to have a good reaction; sell a hundred of each for me."

Trades based on thinks seldom pan out well. The selection of two or three stocks by guesswork instead of one by reason and analysis explains many of the public's losses. If a trader wishes to trade in three hundred shares, let him sell that quantity of the stock **Concentrate** which he knows most about, or which is entitled to the greatest decline. Unless he is playing the long swing he injures his chances by trading in a lot of stocks at once. It's like chasing a drove of pigs—while you're watching this one the others get away.

Better to concentrate on one or two stocks and study them exhaustively. You will find that what applies to one does not always fit the other: each must be judged on its own merits. The varying price levels, volumes, percentage of floating supply, investment values, the manipulation and other factors, all tend to produce a different combination in each particular case.

# III.   The Stock List Analyzed

The Best
Stock Now

I N the last chapter we referred to Union Pacific as the most desirable stock for active trading. The "Analyst" informs us that he once made a composite chart of the principal active stocks, for the purpose of ascertaining which, in its daily fluctuations, followed the course of the general market most accurately. He found Union Pacific was what might be called the market backbone, while the others, especially Reading, frequently showed erratic tendencies, running up or down, more or less contrary to the general trend. Of all the issues under inspection, none possessed the all-around steadiness and general desirability for trading purposes displayed by Union Pacific.

But the Tape Reader, even if he decides to operate exclusively in one stock, cannot close his eyes to what is going on in others. Frequent opportunities occur elsewhere. In proof of this, take the market in the early fall of 1907: Union Pacific was the leader throughout the rise from below 150 to 167⅝. For three or four days before this advance culminated, heavy selling occurred in Reading, St. Paul, Copper, Steel and Smelters, under cover of the strength in Union. This made the turning point of the market as clear as daylight. One had only to go short of Reading and await the break, or he could have played Union with a close stop, knowing that the whole market would collapse as soon as Union turned downward. When the liquidation in other stocks was completed, Union stopped advancing, the supporting orders were withdrawn, and the "pre-election break" took place. This amounted to over 20 points in Union, with proportionate declines in the rest of the list.

The operator who was watching only Union would have been surprised at this; but had he viewed the market as a complete organism he must have seen what was coming. Knowing the point of distribution, he would be on the lookout for the accumulation which must follow, or at least the level where support would be forthcoming. Had he been expert enough to detect this, quick money could have been made on the subsequent rally.

**View the Market Broadly**

While Union Pacific at present constitutes the backbone, this important member is only one part of the market body, which after all is very like the physical structure of a human being.

To get this point clearly in mind, let us draw on our imaginations a little:

Union is strong and advancing; suddenly New York Central develops an attack of gout; Consolidated Gas goes off on a spree; American Ice becomes nauseatingly weak; Southern Railway develops typhoid; Great Western cannot meet expenses, and is prostrated. There may be nothing at all the matter with the backbone, but its strength will be affected by sickness or excesses among the other members.

**Sympathetic Movements**

A bad break may come in Brooklyn Rapid Transit, occasioned by some political attack, or other purely local influence. This cannot possibly affect the business of the grangers, transcontinentals, or coalers, yet St. Paul, Union, and Reading decline as much as B. R. T. A person whose finger is crushed will sometimes faint from the shock to his nervous system, although the injured member will in no wise affect the other members or functions of the body.

The time-worn illustration of the chain which is as strong as its weakest link, will not serve. When the weak link breaks the chain is in two parts, each part being as strong as its weakest link. The market does not break in two, even when it receives a severe blow. If something occurs in the nature of disaster, whereby the money situation, investment demand, public sentiment, and corporate earning power are deeply affected, a tremendous break may occur, but there is always a level, even in a panic, where buying power becomes strong enough to produce a rally or a permanent upturn.

The Tape Reader must endeavor to operate in that stock which combines the widest swings with the broadest market; he may therefore frequently find it to his advantage to switch temporarily into other issues which seem to offer the quickest and surest profits. It is necessary for us to become familiar with the characteristics of the principal speculative mediums that we may judge their advantages in this respect, as well as their weight and bearing upon a given market situation.

The market is made by the minds of many men. The state of these minds is reflected in the prices of securities in which their owners operate. Let us examine some of the individuals, as well as the influences behind certain stocks and groups of stocks in their various relationships. This will, in a sense, enable us to measure their respective power to affect the whole list or the specific issue in which we decide to operate.

**The Market is Mental**

The market leaders are, as already stated, Union, Reading, Steel, St. Paul, Amalgamated and Smelters. Manipulators, professionals and the public derive their inspiration largely from the action of these six issues, in which 40 per cent to 80 per cent of the total daily transactions are concentrated. We will therefore designate these as the "Big Six."

**The Big Six**

Four stocks out of the Big Six are chiefly influenced by the operations of what is known as the Harriman-Standard Oil party, the most active members of which are E. H. Harriman, William Rockefeller, H. H. Rogers, and H. C. Frick. Their four stocks are Union, Reading, St. Paul, and Amalgamated. Of the other two, Smelters is handled by the Guggenheims, while Steel is unquestionably swung up and down more by the influence of public sentiment than anything else. Of course the condition of the steel trade forms the basis of important movements in this issue, and occasionally Morgan or some other large interest may take a hand by buying or selling a few hundred thousand shares, but, generally speaking, it is the attitude of the public which chiefly affects the price of Steel common. This should be borne strictly in mind, as it is a valuable guide to the technical position of the market, which frequently turns on the over-bought or oversold condition of the public.

Next in importance come what we will term the Secondary Leaders; viz., those which at times burst into great activity, accompanied by large volume. These are rightly termed Secondary Leaders, because while they seldom influence the Big Six to a marked extent, the less important issues usually fall into line at their initiative.

The principal Secondary Leaders are:

# The Stock List Analyzed

Atchison
Baltimore & Ohio
Brooklyn Rapid Transit       **Secondary**
Colorado Fuel       **Leaders**
Consolidated Gas
Delaware & Hudson
Erie
Great Northern
Northern Pacific
Illinois Central
Louisville & Nashville
Missouri Pacific
New York Central
Pennsylvania
Southern Pacific
Sugar

Another group which we will call the Minor Stocks is comprised of less important issues, mostly low-priced, and embracing many public favorites, such as

American Car & Foundry
Chesapeake & Ohio       **Minor Stocks**
Chicago Great Western
Colorado Southern
Denver & Rio Grande
Interborough
Mexican Central
Missouri, Kansas & Texas
Norfolk & Western
Ontario & Western
Republic Iron & Steel
Rock Island
Southern Railway
Texas Pacific
Wabash

These groups are arranged solely with regard to their present speculative prominence, and their power to influence the general market. Some people, when they see an advance inaugurated in some of the Minor Stocks, such as Chesapeake & Ohio, Ontario & Western, or Rock Island, are led to buy Pennsylvania, Reading and other Primary or Secondary Leaders, on the ground that the latter will be bullishly affected. This sometimes occurs; more often it does not. It is just as fallacious to expect a 5,000-share operator to follow a 100-share trader, or a 100-share man to be influenced by what the 10-share trader is doing.

**Minor Stocks Do Not Lead**

The various stocks in the market are like a gigantic fleet of boats, all hitched together and being towed by the tugs "Money Situation," and "Business Conditions." In the first row of boats are the Big Six; behind them, the Secondary Leaders, the Minors, and the Miscellaneous issues in the order named. It takes time to generate steam and to get the fleet under way. The leaders are first to feel the impulse; the others follow in turn. Should the tugs halt, the fleet will run along for awhile under its own momentum, and there will be a certain amount of bumping, backing and filling. In case the direction of the tugs is changed abruptly, the bumping is apt to be severe. Obviously, those in the rear cannot gain and hold the leadership without an all-around re-adjustment.

The Big Six are representative of America's greatest industries—railroading, steel making, and mining. It is but natural that these stocks should form the principal outlet to the country's speculative tendencies. The Union Pacific and St. Paul systems cover the entire West. Reading, of itself a large railroad property, dominates the coal mining industry; it is so interlaced with other railroads as to typify the Eastern situation. Steel is closely bound up with the state of general business throughout the states, while Amalgamated and Smelters are the controlling factors in copper mining and the smelting industry.

In order that we may consider the re-lationships of the principal stocks on the list, let us further divide the active issues into groups.

Groups

### THE HARRIMAN GROUP.*

Union Pacific, Reading, Southern Pacific, Atchison, Erie, Illinois Central, Pacific Mail, Wheeling and Lake Erie.

### THE STANDARD OIL GROUP.

Amalgamated Copper, Anaconda, Sugar, St. Paul, Consolidated Gas, Corn Products, American Linseed, Brooklyn Union Gas.

---

*The death of Mr. Harriman since the above has changed these groups somewhat.

## THE MORGAN GROUP.

Atlantic Coast Line, Hocking Valley, Louisville & Nashville, Southern Railway, U. S. Steel, General Electric, and Mercantile Marine.

## THE PENNSYLVANIA GROUP.*

Pennsylvania, Pittsburg, Cin. Ch. & St. Louis, Baltimore & Ohio, Chesapeake & Ohio, Norfolk & Western.

## THE HILL GROUP.

Great Northern, Northern Pacific, Great Northern Ore & Pacific Coast.

## THE GOULD GROUP

Missouri Pacific, Denver & Rio Grande, Texas Pacific, Wabash, Western Maryland, St. Louis Southwestern, Western Union, and Colorado Fuel.

## THE VANDERBILT GROUP.

New York Central, Northwest, C., C., C., & St. L.; Lake Erie & Western, N. Y., Chicago & St. L., N. Y. & Harlem, and Delaware & Hudson.

## THE HAWLEY GROUP*.

Colorado & Southern, Minneapolis & St. Louis, Iowa Central, Toledo, St. L. & Western, Chicago & Alton.

## THE MOORE GROUP.

Rock Island, St. L. & San Francisco, American Can.

## THE CANADIAN PACIFIC GROUP.

Canadian Pacific, Minneapolis, St. Paul, S. S. Marie, Duluth, South Shore & Atlantic.

*Chesapeake & Ohio has since become a Hawley property.

THE GUGGENHEIM GROUP.

Am. Smelting, National Lead, Utah Copper.

THE NEW HAVEN GROUP.

New Haven, Ontario & Western.

Arranged according to industries we have the following:

STEEL STOCKS.

U. S. Steel, Am. Steel Foundries, Bethlehem Steel, Colorado Fuel & Iron, Great Northern Ore, Republic Iron & Steel, Sloss-Sheffield, U. S. Cast Iron Pipe & Foundry.

EQUIPMENT STOCKS.

Am. Car & Foundry, Am. Locomotive, N. Y. Air Brake, Pressed Steel Car, Pullman, Railway Steel Springs.

ELECTRICAL STOCKS.

General Electric, Westinghouse, Allis-Chalmers.

COPPER STOCKS.

Amalgamated, Anaconda, Granby, Newhouse, Tennessee, Utah (Am. Smelters is also closely identified with this industry).

TELEGRAPH AND TELEPHONE STOCKS.

Western Union, Mackay Companies, Am. Telegraph & Telephone.

ANTHRACITE STOCKS.

Reading, Erie, Delaware, Lack. & Western, Delaware & Hudson, Ontario & Western, and Pennsylvania.

CHEMICAL STOCKS.

Am. Agricultural Chemical, Virginia-Carolina Chemical, Am. Cotton Oil.

The above are the principal groups. There are, of course, a number of independent railroads, such as Missouri, Kansas & Texas, Kansas City Southern, Chicago Great Western, and Wisconsin Central, besides local traction companies and combines, such as the Ryan-Belmont Group in New York City, including Interborough-Metropolitan, Third Avenue, and Manhattan. These and other public utility stocks, such as Peoples Gas, and Toledo Railway & Light, etc., are governed by local conditions, and do not, as a rule, affect the general list.

**Industrials**

Large industrial concerns like Am. Sugar, Am. Woolen, International Paper, International Harvester, U. S. Rubber, etc., are also affected principally by the state of their respective trades, and carry little weight otherwise.

Having classified the principal active stocks we can now recognize more clearly the forces behind their movements. For instance, if Consolidated Gas suddenly becomes strong and active, we know it will probably affect Brooklyn Union Gas, but there is no reason why the other Standard Oil stocks should advance more than slightly and out of sympathy. But if all the stocks in the Standard Oil group advance in a steady and sustained fashion, we know that these capitalists are engaged in a bull campaign. As these people do not enter deals for a few points it is safe to go

**Sympathetic Relations**

along with them for awhile, or until distribution becomes apparent.

An outbreak of speculation in Colorado Fuel is no bull argument on the other Steel stocks. It usually means that the Gould party is active. If it were based on trade conditions, U. S. Steel would be the first to feel the impetus, which would radiate to the others.

In selecting the most desirable stock out of the Standard Oil group, for instance, the Tape Reader must consider whether conditions favor the greatest activity and volumes in the railroad or industrial field. In the former case, his choice would be St. Paul; in the latter, Amalgamated.

In the Harriman Group, Erie may come out of its rut (as it did during the summer of 1907, when it was selling around 24), and attain leadership among the low-priced stocks. This indicates some important development in Erie; it does not foreshadow a rise in all the Harrimans. But if a strong rise starts in Union Pacific, and Southern Pacific and the others in the group follow consistently, the Tape Reader will get into the leader and stay with it. He will not waste time on Erie, for while it is moving up 5 points, Union Pacific will advance 10 or 15 points, provided it is a genuine Harriman move. Many valuable deductions may be made by studying these groups.

Experience has shown that when a

*A Low-Priced Stock Rarely Leads*

rise commences in Atchison (a Secondary Leader), the Big Six is about done and distribution is taking place, under protection of the strength in Atchison and others in its class. Sugar acts in a

**Indicators**

similar capacity for the Standard Oil group. Professional traders call these stocks "Indicators."

The Harriman and Standard Oil parties work in harmony, their relations in the various properties being closely interwoven.

The Morgan people are comparatively inactive, except at times when they turn over immense quantities of Steel securities. We feel safe in asserting that few manipulative orders emanate from the corner of Wall and Broad. This is also true of the Hill and Pennsylvania groups, except in rare instances, when bankers are bringing out new issues.

The absence of inside manipulation in a stock leaves the way open for pools to operate, and many of the moves that are observed in these groups are produced by a handful of floor or office

**Pools**

operators, who, by joining hands and swinging large quantities, are able to force their stock in the desired direction.

Activity in the Gould group is largely confined to Missouri Pacific and Colorado Fuel, but the others are taken in hand at times, with the exception of Western Union, which is principally held for investment.

### The Stock List Analyzed

Of the Vanderbilts, New York Central is the leader; all the others usually take their cue from it. Neglect is the principal market characteristic of the majority of this group, most of the outstanding shares being locked up in safe deposit boxes. The principal moves are made by those not identified with the Vanderbilts. (It will be noted that Wm. Rockefeller, James Stillman, and some of the Morgan party are directors.) The "Junior" Vanderbilts, such as N. Y., Ch., & St. L., and Lake Erie & Western are poor leaders, and generally unsatisfactory stocks to watch, except as straws, showing the direction of the wind.

With the exception of Chesapeake & Ohio and Colorado & Southern, the Hawley stocks cut very little figure—their movements carry slight significance.

**Subordinate Groups**

The Moore party's principal activities are confined to Rock Island, the influence of which seldom extends beyond its own controlled properties.

The primary market for Canadian Pacific is in London. The movements of its American loop (Minn., St. Paul & S. S. Marie), are not significant. Duluth, South Shore & Atlantic is given a run once or twice a year by the Canadian Pacific following having its headquarters in Montreal.

The Guggenheims are always active in Smelters, and the stock frequently offers splendid trading opportunities. Lead is frequently used as a "chaser," and is often made active when Smelters has completed its run.

New Haven is mainly held by New Englanders for investment. Ontario & Western is popular with small traders; its movements deserve little consideration.

**The Public**

U. S. Steel is swayed by conditions in the steel trade, and the speculative temper of the general public, assisted occasionally by some of the insiders. No other stock on the list is such a true index of the attitude of the public, or the technical position of the market. Including those who own the stock outright, and those who carry it on margin, probably a quarter of a million people here and abroad closely follow its movements. Weekly reports of the steel trade are most carefully scrutinized, and the corporation's earnings and orders on hand minutely studied by thousands.

This great public never sells its favorite short, but carries it "paid for," or on margin until a profit is secured, or until it is shaken or scared out in a violent decline. Hence, if the stock is strong under adverse news, we may infer that public holdings are strongly fortified, and that confidence abounds. If Steel displays more than its share of weakness, an untenable position of the public is indicated.

The other steel stocks are dominated by the giant corporation, and seldom furnish indications of value to the

Tape Readers, except at the end of a long rise.

At this point public sentiment becomes intensely bullish and spreads itself in the low-priced speculative shares. Insiders in the junior steel stocks take advantage of this and are able to advance and find a good market for their holdings.

**Equipment Stocks**

The Equipment Stocks find their chief inspiration in the orders for cars locomotives, etc., placed by the rail roads. These orders are dependent upon general business conditions. Consequently the equipment issues can seldom be expected to do more than follow the trend of prosperity or depression.

We have thus introduced ourselves to the principal speculative mediums and their families, each of which, upon closer acquaintance, seems to have a sort of personality. If we stand in a room with fifty or a hundred people, all of whom we know, as regards their chief motives and characteristics, we can form definite ideas as to their probable actions under a given set of circumstances. This would be impossible among strangers.

So it becomes the Tape Reader to acquaint himself with the most minute details pertaining to these market identities, also with the habits, motives and methods of the men who make the principal moves on the Stock Exchange chess-board.

**Knowledge of Details**

# IV. Stop Orders, Trading Rules, &c.

WHEN a person contemplates an extensive trip, one of the first things taken into account is the expense—that which cannot be avoided. In planning our excursion into the realms of Tape Reading we must, therefore, carefully weigh the expenses, or, to use a better term, the fixed charges in trading.

Were there no expenses, profit-making would be far easier—profits would merely have to exceed losses. But no matter whether you are a member of the New York Stock Exchange or not, in actual trading profits must exceed losses *and expenses*. These are incurred in every trade, whether it shows a gain or a loss. They consist of:

Commission on 100 shares.....$25.00
Invisible eighth (see TICKER, Vol.
    I, No. 2, p. 17)............ 12.50
Tax on sale ................. 2.00
                   —————
                   $39.50

in addition to interest if the trade is carried over night.

By purchasing a New York Stock Exchange seat, the commission can be reduced to $1 per hundred shares, bought and sold the same day, or $3.12½ if carried over night. This advantage is partly offset by interest on the money involved, dues, assessments, etc., which amount to nearly $5,000 per annum on a seat costing $75,000.

The invisible eighth is a factor which no one—not even a member—can overcome. Nor can the tax be legitimately avoided.

**The Invisible Eighth**

The Tape Reader who is a non-member must, therefore, realize that *the instant he gives an order* to go long or short 100 shares, *he has lost* $39.50. In order that he may not fool himself, he should add his commissions (¼%) to his purchase price, or deduct them from his selling price *immediately*. People who boast of their profits usually forget to deduct expenses. Yet it is this insidious item which frequently throws the net result over to the debit side.

The expression is frequently heard, "I got out even, except the commissions," the speaker evidently scorning such a trifling consideration. This sort of self-deception is ruinous, as will be seen by computing the fixed charges on 10 trades—$395—or on 20 trades—$790. Bear in mind that a loss of $39.50 on the first trade leaves double that amount—$79—to be made on the second trade before a dollar of profit is secured.

It therefore appears that the Tape Reader's problem is not only to eliminate losses, but to cover his expenses as quickly as may be. If he has a couple of points profit in a long trade, there is no reason why he should let the stock run back below his net buying price. Here circumstances seem to call for a stop order, so that no matter what happens, he will not be compelled to pay out money. This stop should not be thrust in when net cost is too close to the market price. Reactions must be allowed for.

**Use of Stop Orders**

A Tape Reader is essentially one who follows the immediate trend. An expert can readily distinguish between a change of trend and a reaction. When his mental barometer indicates a change he does not wait for a stop order to be caught, but cleans house or reverses his position in a twinkling. The stop order at net cost is, therefore, of advantage only in case of a reversal which is sudden, pronounced, and with no forewarning.

A stop should also be placed if the operator is obliged to leave the tape for more than a moment, or if the ticker gets out of order. While he has his eye on the tape the market will tell him what to do. The moment this condition does not exist he must act as he would if temporarily stricken blind —he must protect himself from forces which may assail him in the dark.

I know a trader who once bought 500 shares of Sugar and then went out to lunch. He paid 25 cents for what he ate, but on returning to the tape he found the total cost of that lunch was $5,000.25. He had left no stop order, Sugar was down ten points, and his broker wore a MM (more margin button) in his lapel.

The ticker has a habit of becoming incoherent at the most critical points. Curse it as he may, it will resume printing intelligibly when the trouble is overcome—not before. As the loss of even a few inches of quotations may be important, a stop should be placed at once and left in until the flow of prices is resumed.

**Accidents**

If a trade is carried over night, a stop should be entered against the possibility of accident to the market or the trader. An important event may develop before the next day's opening by which the stock will be violently affected. The trader may be taken ill, be delayed in arrival, or in some way become incapacitated. A certain allowance must be made for accidents of every kind.

·As to where the stop should be placed under such conditions, this depends upon circumstances. The con-

sénsus of shrewd and experienced traders is in favor of two points maximum gross loss on any one trade.
This is purely arbitrary, however. The
Tape Reader knows, as a rule, what to
do when he is at the tape, but if he
is separated from the market by any
contingency, he will be obliged to fall
back upon the arbitrary stop.

**Points of
Resistance**

A closer stop may be obtained by
noting the "points of resistance"—the
levels at which the market turns after
a reaction. For example, if you are
short at 130 and the stock breaks to
128, rallies to 129, and then turns
down again, the point of resistance is
129. In case of temporary absence or
interruption to the service, a good
stop would be 129⅛ or 129¼. These
"points of resistance" will be more
fully discussed later.

**Automatic
Stops**

If the operator wishes to use an automatic stop, a very good method is
this: Suppose the initial trade is
made with a one-point stop. For
every ⅛ the stock moves in your favor,
change the stop to correspond, so that
the stop is never more nor less than
one point away from the extreme market price. This gradually and automatically reduces the risk, and if the
Tape Reader be at all skilful, his profits must exceed losses. As soon as
the stop is thus raised to cover commissions, it would seem best not to
make it automatic thereafter, but let

the market develop its own stop or signal to get out.

One trouble with this kind of a stop is that it interferes with the free play of judgment. A homely illustration will explain why: A tall woman and a short man attempt to cross a street. An automobile approaches. The woman sees that there is ample time in which to cross, but he has her by the arm and being undecided himself, backs and fills, first pushing, then pulling her by the arm until they finally return to the curb, after a hairbreadth escape. Left to herself, she would have known exactly what to do.

It is the same with the Tape Reader. He is hampered by an automatic stop. It is best that he be free to act as his judgment dictates, without feeling compelled by a prior resolution to act according to a hard and fast rule.

There is another time when the stop order is of value to the Tape Reader, viz., when his indications are not clearly defined. The original commitment should, of course, be made only when the trend is positively indicated, but situations will develop when he will be uncertain whether to stand pat, close out, or reverse his position. At such a time it seems better to push the stop up to a point as close as possible to the market price, without choking off the trade. By this we mean a reasonable area should be al-

Uncertainty

lowed for temporary fluctuations. If the stock emerges from its uncertainty by going in the desired direction, the stop can be changed or cancelled. If its trend becomes adverse, the trade is automatically closed.

**Fear**

Fear, hesitation and uncertainty are deadly enemies of the Tape Reader. The chief cause of fear is over-trading. Therefore commitments should be no greater than can be borne by one's susceptibility in this respect.

**Hesitation**

Hesitation must be overcome by self training. To observe a positive indication and not act upon it is fatal —more so in closing than in opening a trade. The appearance of a definite indication should be immediately followed by an order. Seconds are often more valuable than minutes. The Tape Reader is not the captain—he is but the engineer who controls the machinery. The Tape is the pilot and the engineer must obey orders with promptness and precision.

Uncertainty may be reduced by the use of stops as above, or by closing a trade whenever one's course is not entirely clear.

We have defined a Tape Reader as one who follows the immediate trend. This means that he pursues the line of least resistance. He goes *with* the market—he does not buck it. The operator who opposes the immediate trend pits his judgment and his hundred or more shares against the world's supply or demand and the weight of its millions of shares. Armed with a broom, he is trying to stay the incoming tide.

When he goes *with* the trend, the forces of supply, demand and manipulation are working for and with him.

A market which swings within a radius of a couple of points cannot be said to have a trend, and is a good one for the Tape Reader to avoid. The reason is: Unless he catches the extremes of the little swings, he cannot pay commissions, take occasional losses and come out ahead. No yacht can win in a dead calm. As it costs him nearly half a point to trade, each risk should contain a probable two to five points profit, or it is not justified.

**Quiet Markets**

A mechanical engineer, given the weight of an object, the force of the blow which strikes it, and the element through which it must pass, can figure approximately how far the object will be driven. So the Tape Reader, by gauging the impetus or the energy with which a stock starts and sustains a movement, decides whether it is likely to travel far enough to warrant his going with it—whether it will pay its expenses and remunerate him for his boldness.

The ordinary tip-trading speculator gulps a point or two profit and disdains a loss, unless it is big enough to strangle him. The Tape Reader must do the opposite—he must cut out every possible eighth loss and search for chances to make three, five and ten points. He does not have to grasp everything that looks like an opportunity. It is not necessary for him to be in the market continuously. He chooses only the best of what the tape offers.

His original risks can be gradually effaced by clever arrangement of stop orders when a stock goes his way. He may keep these in his head or put them on the floor. For my own part I prefer, having decided upon a danger point, to maintain a mental stop and when the price is reached close the trade at the market. Reason: There may be ground for a change of plan or opinion at the last moment; if a stop is on the floor it takes time to cancel or change it, hence there is a period of a few minutes when the operator does not know where he stands. By using mental stops and market orders he always knows where he stands, except as regards the prices at which his orders are executed. The main consideration is, he knows whether he is in or out.

The placing of stops is most effectual and scientific when indicated by the market itself. An example of this is as follows:

**Mental Stops**

—Stop raised to
129⅝.

—Buying point,
128¾.

—Initial stop,
127⅞.

Here a stock, fluctuating between 128 and 129, gives a buying indication at 128¾. Obviously, if the indication is true, the price will not again break 128, having met buying sufficiently strong to turn it up twice from that figure and a third time from 128⅛. The fact that it did not touch 128 on the last down swing forecasts a higher up swing; it shows that the downward pressure was not so strong and the demand slightly more urgent. In other words, the point of resistance was raised ⅛. Having bought .at

128¾, the stop is placed at 127⅞, which is ¼ below the last point of resistance.

**Market Indication of Stops**

The stock goes above its previous ·top (129⅛) and continues to 130¾. At any time after it has crossed 130 the operator may raise his stop to cost plus commission (129). The stock reacts at 129⅞, then continues the advance to above 131. As soon as a new high point is reached the stop is raised to 129⅝, as 129⅞ was the point of resistance on the dip.

In such a case the initial risk was ⅞ plus commissions, etc., the market giving a well defined stop point, making an arbitrary stop not only unnecessary but expensive. The illustration is given in chart form, but the experienced Tape Reader generally carries these swings in his head. A series of higher tops and bottoms are made in a pronounced up swing and the reverse in a down swing.

Arbitrary stops may, of course, be used at any time, especially if one wishes to clinch a substantial profit, but until a stock gets away from the price at which it was entered, it seems best to use the stops it develops for itself.

If the operator is shaken out of his holdings immediately after entering the trade, it does not prove his judgment in error. Some accident may have happened, some untoward devel-

opment in a particular issue, of sufficient weight to affect the rest of the
list. It is these unknown quantities
that make the limitation of losses
most important. In such a case it
would be folly to change the stop so
that the risk is increased. This, while
customary with the public, is something a Tape Reader seldom does.
Each trade is made on its own basis,
and for certain definite reasons. At
the outset the amount of risk should
be decided upon, and, except in very
rare instances, should not be changed,
except on the side of profit. The Tape
Reader must eliminate, not enhance,
his risk.

**No Increase of Risk**

Averaging does not come within the
province of the Tape Reader. Averaging is groping for the top or bottom.
The Tape Reader must not grope. He
must see and know, or he should not
act.

It is impossible to fix a rule govern-
ing the amount of profit the operator
should accept. In a general way, there
should be no limit set as to the profits. A deal, when entered, may look
as though it would yield three or four
points, but if the strength increases
with the advance it may run ten
points before there is any sign of a
halt.

We wish our readers to bear fully
in mind that these recommendations
and suggestions are not to be consid-

ered final or inflexible. It is not our aim to assume the role of an oracle. Rather, we are reasoning things out on paper, and as we progress in these studies and apply these tentative rules to the tape, in actual or paper trading, we shall probably have occasion to modify some of our conclusions.

**Closing Trades**

A Tape Reader must close a trade (1) when the tape tells him to close; (2) when his stop is caught; (3) when his position is not clear; (4) when he has a large or satisfactory profit.

The first and most important reason for closing a trade is: The tape says so. This indication may appear in various forms. Assuming that one is trading in a leader like Union Pacific or Reading, the warning may come in the stock itself. Within the ribbon of sales recorded on the tape, there runs the fine silken thread of the trend. It is clearly distinguishable to one sufficiently versed in the art of Tape Reading, and, for reasons previously explained, is most readily observed in the leaders. Hence when one is short of Union Pacific and this thread suddenly indicates that the market has turned upward, it is folly to remain short. Not only must one cover quickly, but if the power of the movement is sufficient to warrant the risk, the operator must go long. In a market of sufficient breadth and swing, the Tape Reader will find that when it is

time to close a trade, it is usually time
to reverse his position. One must
have the flexibility of whalebone, and
entertain no rigid opinion. He must
obey the tape implicitly.

The indication to close a trade may
come from another stock, several
stocks or the general market. For example, on January 4th this year, the
day of the Supreme Court decision in
Consolidated Gas, suppose the operator was long of Union Pacific at 11
o'clock, having paid therefor 182¾.

Between 11 and 12 o'clock Union
rallied to 183½, and Reading, which
was more active, to 144. Just before,
and immediately after, the noon hour,
tremendous transactions took place in
Reading, over 50,000 shares changing
hands within three-quarters of a point.
These may have been largely wash
sales, accompanied by inside selling;
it is impossible to tell. If they were
not, the inference is that considerable
buying power developed in Reading at
this level and was met by selling
heavy enough to supply all bidders
and prevent the stock advancing above
144⅜. Large quantities coming within a small range indicated either one
of two things: (1) That considerable
buying power suddenly developed at
this point, and the insiders chose to
check it or to take advantage of the
opportunity to unload. (2) The dem-
onstration in Reading may have been

intended to distract attention from other stocks in which large operators were unloading. (There is no special evidence of this, except in New York Central.)

If the selling is not sufficient to check the upward move, the market for Reading will absorb all that is offered and advance, now or later, to a higher level, but in this case the selling was more effectual than the buying, and Reading fell back, warning the operator that the temporary leader on the bull side of the market had met with defeat.

**A Check to Reading**

If a stock or the whole market cannot be advanced, the assumption is that it will decline—a market seldom stands still. At this point the operator was, therefore, on the lookout for a slump.

Reading subsided, in small lots, back to 143⅞. Union Pacific, after selling at 183⅝, declined to 183¼. Both stocks developed dullness, and the whole market became more or less without feature.

Suddenly Union Pacific came 183⅛. 500.183.200.182⅞.500.¾, indicating not only a lack of demand, but remarkably poor support. Immediately following this, New York Central, which sold only a few minutes before 400.-131½ came 131.1700.130¼.500.130. This demonstrated that the market was remarkably hollow and in a position to develop great weakness. The large quantities of New York Central at the low figure, after a running decline of a point and one-half, showed that there was not only an absence of supporting orders, but that sellers were obliged to make great concessions in order to dispose of their holdings. The quantities, especially in view of the narrowness of the market, proved that the sellers were not small fry.

Coupled with the wet blanket put on Reading and the poor support in Union Pacific, this weakness in New York Central was another advance notice of a decline. On any further indication he must be ready to jump out of his long stock and get short of the market.

**Catching the Cue**

While waiting for his cue, the Tape Reader has time to consider which stock among the leaders is the most desirable for selling. He quickly chooses Reading, on the ground that the large lots which have apparently been distributed around 144 will probably come into the market as soon as weakness develops. Reason: The outside public generally buys on just such bulges as the one which has taken place in Reading. A large volume, even if accompanied by only a fractional advance, has the effect of making the ordinary trader intensely bullish, the result being that he bites off a lot of long stock at the top of the

**Public Buying**

Buying at
the Top

bulge. This is exactly what the manipulator wishes him to do. We have all heard people boast that their purchase was at the top eighth and that it had the effect of turning the stock down. Those who make their purchases after this fashion are quickest to become scared at the first appearance of weakness, and throw overboard what they have bought. In choosing Reading, therefore, the Tape Reader is picking out the stock in which he is likely to have the most help on the bear side.

At 12.30 the market is standing still, the majority of transactions being in small lots and at only fractional changes. Reading shows the effect of the recent unloading. It is coming out 500.143¾.500.⅝.400.½.¾. The operator realizes that Reading is probably a short sale right here, with a stop order at 144½ or ⅝, on the ground that the bulls must have an extraordinary amount of latent buying power in order to push the stock above its former top, where, at every eighth advance over 144⅜, they will encounter a considerable portion of 50,000 shares. This reasoning, however, is all aside from our main argument, which is to show how the cue to get out will be given by stocks other than that in which the operator is working.

Union Pacific shows on the tape in small lots at 182¾; New York Central 1100.130.900.⅜. The rest of the market seems to have all the snap and ginger taken out of it and the operator does not like his position on the long side. He has no definite indication to sell short, however, but feeling that his chances on the long side have been reduced to practically nil by the weak undertone of the market, he therefore **Closing Out** gets out of his Union Pacific and waits until the tape tells him to sell Reading short.

Union Pacific weakens to 182⅝. The others slide off fractionally. The weakness is not positive enough to forecast any big break, so he continues to wait. There are 1800 shares of Union altogether at 182⅝, followed by 3000 at 182½. Other stocks respond and the market looks more bearish.

Consolidated Gas comes 163¾.¼. 163. This is the first sign of activity in the stock, but the move is nothing unusual for Gas, as its fluctuations are generally wide and erratic. The balance of the list rallies a fraction. Gas comes 162½.¾.500.162¼. At this point Gas, which has been very dull heretofore, now forces itself, by its decline and weakness, upon the notice of the operator. He begins to look upon the stock as the possible shears which will cut the thread of the market and let everything down.

12.45—Gas 500.161½ . It is very **Break** weak. The balance of the list is **in Gas** steady, Union Pacific 182⅝, Central 130⅜, Reading 143¾. There is a fractional rally — Union Pacific to 182⅞ and Gas to 162. Plenty of Central for sale around 130; Reading is 143½.

The rally peters out. There is a gradual weakening all around, but the Tape Reader cannot go with the trend until he is sure of a big swing. Central comes 129¾, showing that after all the buyers at 130 are filled up considerable stock is still for sale. The others show only in small lots. The market is on the verge of a decline; it is where a push or a jar of any sort will start it down. Union Pacific is heavy at 182½.300.⅜.200.½, Reading 143½.⅜.1000½, Central 2000.130.800. ⅛.

**The Thrust**

Here is the thrust he has been looking for! Gas 163¾.200.½.400.161.300. 160½.400.160! He waits no longer, but gives an order to sell Reading short at the market. They are all on the run now, Reading 143½.600.⅜. 1300.¼. Central 130.129½, Gas 500, 159½. Something very rotten about Gas and it's a cinch to sell it short if you don't mind trading in a buzz-saw stock.

The market breaks so rapidly that he does not get over 142¾ for his Reading, but he is short not far from the top of what looks like a wide open break.

## Stop Orders, Trading Rules, &c.

Everything is slumping now—Steel, Smelters, Southern Pacific, St. Paul. Union Pacific is down to 181⅝, and the rest in proportion.

Gas 158½.158.300.157.156.155.154.153 and the rest "come tumbling after." Reading 141⅜.500.¼.400.141. 1 4 0 ¾ .500.½.200.140.600.139¾.500.⅝. Union 181.180⅞.¾.½.¼.600.⅛.5 0 0. 180.179¾.500.½.300.¼, Central 127½.

The Break

The above illustrates some of the workings of a Tape Reader's mind; also how a break in a stock, entirely foreign to that which is being traded in, will furnish the indication to get out and go short of one stock or another.

The indication to close a trade may come from the general market where the trend is clearly developed throughout the list, all stocks working in complete harmony. One of the best indications in this line is the strength or weakness on rallies and reactions. These will be discussed in a subsequent issue.

Of course the break in Gas, which finally touched 138, is due to the Supreme Court decision, which was announced on the news tickers at 1.1 P. M., but, as is usually the case, the tape told the news many mintues before anything else. This is one of the advantages of getting your news from the first place where it is reflected. Other people who wait for such infor-

News From the Tape

mation to sift through telephone and telegraph wires and reach them by the roundabout way of news tickers or word of mouth, are working under a tremendous handicap.

That not even the insiders knew what the decision was to be is shown in the dullness of the stock all morning. Those who heard the decision in the Supreme Court chamber doubtless did the double-quick to the telephone and sold the stock short. Their sales showed on the tape before the news arrived in New York. Tape Readers were, therefore, first to be notified. They were short before the Street knew what had happened.

# V.  Volumes and Their Significance

AS the whole object of these studies is to learn to read what the
tape says, I will now explain a
point which is probably one of
the most valuable in the practice of the
art.  This must be known and understood
before we proceed, otherwise the explanations cannot be made clear.

First of all, we must recognize that
the market for any stock—at whatever
level it may be—is composed of two
sides, represented by the bid and the
asked price.  Please remember that the
last sale is something entirely different
from the market price.  If Steel has just
sold at 50, this figure represents what
*has* happened.  It is history.  The *market price* of Steel is either 49⅛@50 or
50@50⅛.  *The bid and asked prices
combined form the market price.*

This market price is like a pair of
scales, and the volume of stock thrown
by sellers and reached for by purchasers
shows toward which side the prepon-
derance of weight has momentarily shift-
ed.  For example, when the tape shows

"Market
Price"
Defined

US.

500 . 50 . 1000 . ⅛ . 50 . 1500 . ⅛

the market price is 50@⅛, and the large volumes are on the up side. In these four transactions there are 700 shares sold at 50 against 2,500 taken at 50⅛, proving that *at the moment* the buying is more urgent than the selling. The deduction here to be made is that Steel will probably sell at 50¼ before 49⅞. There is no certainty in this, for supply and demand is changing with every second, not only in Steel but in every other stock on the list.

**Advantage of the Leaders**

Here is one advantage in trading in the leaders. The influence of demand or pressure is concentrated or at least strongly felt in the principal stocks. The hand of the dominant power, whether it be an insider, an outside manipulator or the public, is shown in these volumes. Especially is this true in the pivotal stocks, like Union Pacific, Reading and others, which are generally used by the Harriman and Rockefeller parties. The reason is simple. These big fellows cannot put their stocks up or down without trading in enormous amounts. In an advancing market they are obliged to reach up for or bid up their stocks, as, for example:

**U**

182 . 1000 . ⅛ . 200 . 182 . 1500 . ⅛

200¼ . 3500 . ⅜ . 2000 . ½ .

In a case like the following, Union Pacific is being bought on a decline whenever round lots come into the market:

**U**                                                    Examples

200 . 181½ . 2600 . ⅝ . ½ . 200 .

⅜ . ¼ . ⅛ . 4000 . ¼ . 1500 . ⅜ .

Take the opening and subsequent transactions in American Locomotive one day last fall:

| | | |
|---|---|---|
| 200...47¼ | 100...45⅞ | 100...45⅞ |
| 1900...46¾ | 100...46⅛ | 100...46 |
| 100...46⅝ | 100...46 | 600...45⅞ |
| 100...46½ | 200...46¼ | 500...45¾ |
| 100...46⅜ | 100...46⅜ | 200...45⅝ |
| 600...46¼ | 11 A. M. | 100...45½ |
| 100...46⅛ | 300...46⅜ | 100...45⅝ |
| 600...46 | 100...46⅛ | 400...45⅞ |
| 100...45⅞ | 100...46 | 100...45¾ |
| 200...45¾ | 100...45⅞ | 400...45⅝ |
| 100...46 | 100...46 | 100...45¾ |

Here the opening market price was 46¾ @ 47¼, and the buyers of 200 shares "at the market" paid the high price. All bids at 46¾ were then filled. This is proved by the next sale, which is at 46⅝. The big lots thereafter are mostly on the down side, showing that pressure still existed. The indications were, therefore, that the stock would go lower. A lot of 1900 shares in a stock like Locomotive is a large lot; in Union Pacific it would be of frequent occurrence, even in comparatively dull markets.

**Proportional Volumes**

Volumes must be valued in proportion to the activity of the market, as well as the relative activity of that particular issue. No set rule can be established. I have seen a Tape Reader make money by following the lead of a 1000-share lot of Northwest which someone took at a fraction above the last sale. Ordinarily Northwest is a sluggish investment stock, and this size lot appeared as the forerunner of an active speculative demand.

Now let us see what happens on the floor to produce the above-described effect on the tape—let us prove that our theory is correct. A few years ago the control of a certain railroad was being bought on the floor of the New York Stock Exchange. One house was given all the orders, with instructions to distribute them and conceal the buying as much as possible. The original order

for the day would read, "Take everything that is offered up to 38." As 38
was about 3 points above the market of
the day before, this left considerable lee-
way for the broker to whom the buying
order was entrusted.

He would instruct his floor broker as
follows: "The stock closed last night
at 35. You take everything offered up
to 35½ and then report to me how
things stand. Don't bid for the stock;
just take it as it is offered and mark it
down whenever you can."

In such a case the floor member stands
in the crowd awaiting the opening. On
the instant of ten o'clock the chairman's
gavel strikes and the crowd begins yell-
ing. Someone offers "2000 at an eighth."
Another broker says "Five for five hundred." Our broker takes the 2000 at ⅛,
then offers it at ⅛ himself, so as to keep
the price down. Others then offer one
or two hundred shares at ⅛, so he with-
draws his offer, as he wishes to accumulate and only offers or sells when it helps
him buy more, or puts the price down.
The buyer at 35 has 300 shares of his
lot cancelled, so he alters his bid to "35
for two hundred." The other sellers
supply him and he then bids "⅞ for a
hundred." Our broker sells him 100 at
⅞ just to get the market down. Someone comes in with "a thousand at five."
Our broker says, "I'll take it." Five
hundred more is offered at ⅛. This he
also takes.

On the
Floor

Let us see how the tape records these transactions:

---

2000 . 35⅛ . 200 . 35 . 34⅞

---

. 1000 . 35 . 500 . ⅛

---

The Tape Reader interprets this: Opening bid and asked price was probably 35@⅛; someone took the large lot at the high price. The two sales following were in small lots, showing light pressure. The 1000@35 after 34⅞ shows that on the ⅞@5 market the buyer took the stock at the offered price and followed it up by taking 500 more at the eighth. The weight is on the up side and it does not matter whether the buyer is one individual or a dozen, the momentary trend is upward.

**Marking Down**

To get the opposite side, let us suppose a manipulator is desirous of depressing a stock. This can be accomplished by offering and selling more than there is a demand for, or by coaxing or frightening other holders into throwing over their shares. It makes no difference whose stock is sold; "The Lord is on the side of the heaviest battalions," as Addison Cammock used to say. When a manipulator puts a broker into a crowd with orders to mark it down, the broker supplies all bids and then offers it down to the objective point or until he meets resistance too strong for him to overcome without the loss of a large block of stock.

The issue in question is selling around 80, we will say, and the broker's orders are to "put it to 77." Going into the crowd, he finds 500 wanted at 79⅞ and 300 offered at 80. Last sale, 100 at 80.

"I'll sell you that five hundred at seven-eighths. A thousand or any part at three-quarters" he shouts.

"I'll take two hundred at three-quarters," says another broker.

"A half for five hundred" yells a voice. "Sold!" is the response. "A half for five hundred more." "Sold!" "That's a thousand I sold you at a half. Five hundred at three-eighths!"

"I'll take a hundred at three-eighths," comes a voice.

"You're on!" is the reply.

"Quarter for five hundred."

"Sold!" is the quick response.

His pounding of the stock would reveal itself on the tape as follows:

---

X

80 . 500 . 79⅞ . 200 . ¾

---

1000 . ½ . ⅜ . 500 . ¼

---

If he met strong resistance at 79 it would appear on the tape something like this:

X

79⅛ . 1000 . 79 . 500 . 79 . 800 . 79 . 300

. ⅛    1000 . 79 . 500 . ¼ . ⅜ . 200 . ½

**Resistance**    showing that at 79 there was a demand for more than he was willing to supply (there might have been 10,000 shares wanted at 79).

Frequently a broker meeting such an obstacle will leave the crowd long enough to 'phone his principal. His departure opens the way for a rally, as the stock is no longer under pressure, and the large buying order at 79 is something for floor traders to fall back on. So those in the crowd bid it up to ½ in hopes of scalping a fraction on the long side.

Take another case where two brokers are put into the crowd—one to depress the stock and the other to accumulate it. They play into each other's hands, and the tape makes the following report of what happens:

X

80⅛ . 80 . 200 . 79⅞ . ¾ . 1000 . ⅞

¾    200 . ⅝ . 500 . ¾ . 300 . ¾ . ½ .

⅜ . 1500 . ½ . ⅜ . 500 . ¼ . ⅛ .

## Volumes and Their Significance

Were we on the floor we should see one broker offering the stock down, while the other grabbed every round lot that appeared. We cannot tell how far down the stock will be put, but when these indications appear it makes us watch closely for the turning point, which is our time to buy.

So far as the Tape Reader is concerned, he does not care whether the move is made by a manipulator, a group of floor traders, the public or a combination of all.

The figures on the tape represent the consensus of opinion, the effect of manipulation and the supply and demand, all combined into concrete units. That is why tape indications are more reliable than what anyone hears, knows or thinks.

With this idea of the pair of scales clearly implanted in our minds, we scan the tape, mentally weighing the leaders in our effort to learn on which side the tendency is strongest. Not a detail must escape our notice. A sudden demand or a burst of liquidation may enable us to form a new plan, revise an old one or bid us wait. **A Pair of Scales**

These volume indications are not always clear. Nor are they infallible. It does not do to rely upon the indications of any one stock to the exclusion of the rest. There was a time, in September, 1908, when certain stocks (Union and Reading, if memory is correct) were being rushed up, while the volume indications in the other active stocks showed clearly that they were being distributed as fast as the market would take them. This happens very frequently on a large or small scale. Especially is it apparent at the turning point of a big swing where accumulation or distribution requires some days to complete.

**Study of Volumes**

Volumes can be studied from the reports printed in the New York *Evening Sun* or the *Wall Street Journal,* but the real way to study them is from the tape. If one is unable to spend five hours a day at the tape while the ticker is in operation, he can arrange with one of the boys in his broker's office to wind the tape up each day and save it for him. This is done most expeditiously by using an automatic reel, which can be had at any store where telegraph instruments are sold. The tape can then be taken home and studied at leisure. A second reel in the study makes it easy to unwind, after which the tape can be made to run across one's desk just as though it were coming from the ticker.

In studying under these conditions do not let yourself be deceived as to your ability to make money on paper. Imaginary trades prove nothing in Tape Reading. The way to test your powers is to get into the game. Let it be on as small a scale as you like, but make actual trades with real money.

There are times when the foregoing

rule of volumes indicates almost the reverse of what we have explained. One of these instances was described in our last chapter. In this case the transactions in Reading suddenly swelled out of all proportion to the rest of the market and its own previous volume. Notwithstanding the predominance of apparent demand, the resistance offered (whether legitimate or artificial) became too great for the stock to overcome, and it fell back from 144⅜. On the way up these volumes alone suggested a purchase, but the tape showed abnormal transactions accompanied by poor response from the rest of the list. This suggested manipulation and warned the operator to be cautious on the bull side. The volume in Reading was sustained even after the stock reacted, but the large lots were evidently thrown over at the bid prices. On the way up the volumes were nearly all on the up side and the small lots on the down side. After 144⅜ was reached the large lots were on the down side and the small lots on the up.

**Poor Response**

It is just as important to study the small as the large lots. The smaller quantities are like the feathers on an arrow—they indicate that the business part of the arrow is at the other end. In other words, the smaller lots keep one constantly informed as to what fraction forms the other side of the market. To illustrate: During the first five trades in

**The Small Lots**

## Tape Reading

```
 700...143⅝
 500...143¾
5000...143⅝
1700...143¾
 200...143⅝
4300...143¾
3700...143⅞
 100...144
    12 M.
5000...144
1300...143⅞
3000...144
5000...144⅛
2100...144¼
2200...144⅛
3500...144¼
4000...144⅜
3000...144¼
2500...144⅛
3500...144
 400...144⅛
1000...144
 500...144⅛
1100...144
2000...143⅞
2500...143¾
1000...143⅝
```

Turning point in Reading, morning of Jan. 4, 1909—
the day of the Consolidated Gas collapse

Reading, recorded above, the market quotation is shown to have been ⅝@¾; it then changed to ¾@⅞ and again to ⅞@4. On the way down it got to be 4@⅛, and at this level the small lots were particularly valuable in showing the pressure which existed.

**Volumes at Turning Points**

Stocks like Union and Reading usually make this sort of a turning point on a volume of from 25,000 to 50,000 shares. That is, when they meet with opposition on an advance or a decline it must be in some such quantity in order to stem the tide.

Walk into the hilly country and you will probably find a small rivulet running quietly on its way. The stream is so tiny that you can place your hand in its course and the water will back up. In five minutes, however, it overcomes this resistance by going over or around your hand. You fetch a shovel, pile dirt in its path, pack it down hard and say, "There, I've dammed you." But you haven't at all, for the next day you find your pile of dirt washed away. You bring cartloads of dirt and build a substantial dam, and the flow is finally held in check.

It is the same with an individual stock or the market. Prices follow the line of least resistance. If Reading is going up someone may throw 10,000 shares in its path without perceptible effect. Another lot of 20,000 shares follows; the stock halts, but finally overcomes the obstacle. The seller gives another order—this time 30,000 shares more are thrown on the market. If there are 30,100 shares wanted at that level, the stock will break through and go higher; if only 29,900 shares are needed to fill all bids, the price will recede because demand has been overcome by supply.

*Line of Least Resistance*

It looks as though something like this happened in Reading on the occasion referred to. Whether or not manipulative orders predominated does not change the

## Tape Reading

Volume Study in Union Pacific, Showing 39,300 Shares Sold from 149¾ to 150, Checking the Rise

| | | | | | |
|---|---|---|---|---|---|
| 200 | ......147⅞ | 1400 | ......147⅞ | 1100 | ......148¾ |
| 6500 | ...{ 147½ | 1500 | ......147¾ | 200 | ......148⅝ |
| | 146¾ | 2000 sld. | ...147⅜ | 600 | ......148½ |
| 100 | ......147 | 500 | ......147¾ | 100 | ......148⅝ |
| 500 | ......146⅞ | 200 | ......147⅝ | 600 | ......148½ |
| 1200 | ......146¾ | 200 | ......147¾ | 100 | ......148⅝ |
| 1000 | ......146⅞ | 1400 | ......147⅝ | 1200 | ......148½ |
| 1000 | ......147 | 1000 | ......147¾ | 100 | ......148⅝ |
| 500 | ......147⅛ | 200 | ......147⅝ | 1700 | ......148¾ |
| 1000 | ......147¼ | 1000 | ......147½ | 2400 | ......148⅝ |
| 1000 | ......147⅜ | 400 | ......147⅝ | 100 | ......148¾ |
| 1000 | ......147¼ | 1000 | ......147½ | 700 | ......148⅝ |
| 500 | ......147⅛ | 600 | ......147⅝ | 100 | ......148¾ |
| 800 | ......147 | 800 | ......147½ | 100 | ......148⅝ |
| 600 | ......146⅞ | 2100 | ......147⅝ | 1100 | ......148¾ |
| 600 | ......147 | 200 | ......147¾ | 1600 | ......148⅞ |
| 400 | ......147½ | 2800 | ......147⅞ | 100 | ......149 |
| 1000 | ......147¼ | 1400 | ......148 | 700 | ......148⅞ |
| 1800 | ......147⅛ | 400 | ......147⅞ | 5700 | ......149 |
| 2600 | ......147¼ | 2100 | ......148 | 4400 | ......149⅛ |
| 1100 | ......147⅜ | 900 | ......147⅞ | 100 | ......149 |
| 1500 | ......147¼ | 1000 | ......148 | 1500 | ......149⅛ |
| 2900 | ......147⅜ | 1800 | ......148½ | 2500 | ......149 |
| 200 | ......147¼ | 700 | ......148¼ | 1300 | ......148⅞ |
| 1100 | ......147⅜ | 400 | ......148⅛ | 1100 | ......149 |
| 1200 | ......147¼ | 2500 | ......148 | 1600 | ......148⅞ |
| 1800 | ......147⅜ | 1300 | ......148½ | 1600 | ......148¾ |
| 500 | ......147½ | 1200 | ......148¼ | 1100 | ......148⅞ |
| 2200 | ......147⅜ | 500 | ......148⅛ | 600 | ......148¾ |
| 2200 | ......147½ | 400 | ......148¼ | 300 | ......148⅝ |
| 500 | ......147⅜ | 2800 | ......148⅜ | 600 | ......148½ |
| 500 | ......147½ | 500 | ......148¼ | 800 | ......148¾ |
| 500 | ......147⅜ | 1200 | ......148⅜ | 500 | ......148½ |
| 3000 | ......147½ | 3500 | ......148¼ | 1000 | ......148⅝ |
| 700 | ......147⅜ | 900 | ......148⅜ | 1200 | ......148¼ |
| 400 | ......147½ | 300 | ......148½ | 500 | ......148⅜ |
| 2400 | ......147⅝ | 700 | ......148⅜ | 3200 | ......148¼ |
| 200 | ......147½ | 100 | ......148¼ | 600 | ......148⅜ |
| 1300 | ......147⅝ | 400 | ......148⅜ | 800 | ......148¼ |
| 1700 | ......147¾ | 400 | ......148¼ | 100 | ......148⅛ |
| 700 | ......147⅝ | 1100 | ......148⅜ | 800 | ......148¼ |
| 500 | ......147¾ | 200 | ......148½ | 900 | ......148⅜ |
| 700 | ......147⅝ | 200 | ......148⅜ | 1700 | ......148¼ |
| 900 | ......147½ | 300 | ......148¼ | 2600 | ......148⅛ |
| 200 | ......147⅝ | 400 | ......148⅛ | 100 | ......148¼ |
| 400 | ......147½ | 1300 | ......148¼ | 100 | ......148⅜ |
| 100 | ......147⅝ | 1500 | ......148⅛ | 300 | ......148¼ |
| 100 | ......147½ | | | 1100 | ......148⅛ |
| 1800 | ......147⅝ | **11 A. M.** | | 400 | ......148 |
| 1000 | ......147½ | 300 | ......148¼ | 500 | ......148⅛ |
| 700 | ......147¾ | 900 | ......148⅜ | | |
| 1300 | ......147½ | 2200 | ......148½ | **12 M.** | |
| 700 | ......147⅜ | 1500 | ......148⅝ | 100 | ......148½ |
| 1000 | ......147½ | 1900 | ......148¾ | 700 | ......148¼ |
| 800 | ......147⅝ | 1700 | ......148⅞ | 100 | ......148¾ |

# Volumes and Their Significance

| | | | | | |
|---|---|---|---|---|---|
| 1200 | 148¼ | 400 | 148⅜ | 500 | 149⅞ |
| 100 | 148½ | 1100 | 148½ | 500 | 149¾ |
| 100 | 148⅝ | 1600 | 148⅝ | 1500 | 149⅞ |
| 1100 | 148½ | 2700 | 148¾ | 100 | 149¾ |
| 100 | 148⅝ | 400 | 148⅞ | 500 | 149⅝ |
| 100 | 148½ | 100 | 148¾ | 1600 | 149¾ |
| 200 | 148⅝ | 1200 | 148⅞ | 1100 | 149⅞ |
| 800 | 148¾ | 600 | 148¾ | 100 | 149¾ |
| 800 | 148½ | 300 | 148⅞ | 500 | 149⅞ |
| 2900 | 148⅝ | 3200 | 149 | 4400 | 149¾ |
| 1100 | 148½ | 300 | 149⅛ | 1000 | 149⅞ |
| 500 | 148⅝ | 3000 | 149¼ | 200 | 149¾ |
| 300 | 148¼ | 1500 | 149⅜ | 100 | 149⅝ |
| 800 | 148⅝ | 800 | 149¼ | 1200 | 149¾ |
| 700 | 148½ | 200 | 149⅛ | 200 | 149⅝ |
| 100 | 148⅝ | 200sld. | 148⅞ | 300 | 149¾ |
| 400 | 148½ | 300 | 149⅛ | 800 | 149⅝ |
| 100 | 148¾ | 700 | 149¼ | 700 | 149½ |
| 1600 | 148⅝ | 100 | 149⅛ | 100 | 149⅜ |
| 1800 | 148¾ | 500 | 149¼ | 1400 | 149¼ |
| 400 | 148⅝ | | | 1200 | 149¼ |
| 400 | 148¾ | **2 P. M.** | | 800 | 149¼ |
| 900 | 148⅝ | | | 1700 | 149⅛ |
| 100 | 148½ | 400 | 149¼ | 2500 | 149 |
| | | 700 | 149⅜ | 100 | 149⅛ |
| **1 P. M.** | | 4300 | 149¼ | 2300 | 149 |
| | | 100 | 149⅛ | 500 | 148⅞ |
| 800 | 148½ | 1300 | 149¼ | 1400 | 148¾ |
| 100 | 148⅞ | 1500 | 149⅜ | 1600 | 149 |
| 200 | 148¼ | 600 | 149¼ | 700 | 148⅞ |
| 100 | 148⅝ | 1700 | 149⅜ | 500 | 148¾ |
| 100 | 148¼ | 600 | 149¼ | 800 | 148⅝ |
| 100 | 148½ | 1600 | 149⅜ | 100 | 148⅝ |
| 600 | 148⅝ | 2800 | 149½ | 400 | 148¾ |
| 100 | 148½ | 1400 | 149⅝ | 2300 | 148⅝ |
| 100 | 148⅝ | 500 | 149¾ | 200 | 148¾ |
| 900 | 148¼ | 600 | 149⅝ | 2800 | 148⅝ |
| 100 | 148⅞ | 10300 | 149¾ | 1200 | 148½ |
| 200 | 148¼ | 5800 | 149⅞ | 200 | 148⅜ |
| 500 | 148¼ | 6000 | 150 | 900 | 148½ |
| 500 | 148⅛ | 1600 | 149⅞ | 1000 | 148⅜ |
| 100 | 148 | 300 | 150 | 400 | 148½ |
| 700 | 148¼ | 800 | 149⅞ | 500 | 148⅝ |
| 800 | 148¼ | 1000 | 149¾ | 1500 | 148¾ |

aspect of the case. In the final shuffling the weight was on the down side.

The public and the floor traders do not stand aside while the manipulator is at work, nor is the reverse true. Everybody's stock looks alike on the tape. The ticker plays no favorites.

When a stream breaks through a dam it goes into new territory. Likewise the breaking through of a stock is significant, for it means that the resistance has been overcome. The stronger the resistance the less likelihood of finding further obstacles in the immediate vicinity—dams are not usually built one behind the other. So when we find a stock emerging into a new field it is best to go with it, especially if, in breaking through it, it carries the rest of the market along.

**A Live Tape**　While much can be learned from the reports printed in the dailies mentioned above, the tape itself is the only real instruction book. A live tape is to be preferred, for the element of speed with which the ticker prints is no small factor. The comparative activity of the market on bulges and breaks is a guide to the technical condition of the market. For instance, during a decline, if the ticker is very active and the volume of sales large, voluntary or compulsory liquidation is indicated. This is emphasized if, on the subsequent rally, the tape moves sluggishly and only small lots appear. In an active bull market the ticker appears to be choked with the volume of sales poured through it on the advances, but on reactions the quantities and the number of impressions decrease until, like the ocean at ebb tide, the market is almost lifeless.

Another indication of the power of a movement is found in the differences between sales of active stocks, for example:

---

U

1000 . 180 . $\frac{1}{8}$ . 500 . $\frac{3}{8}$ . 1000 . $\frac{1}{2}$

---

This shows that there was only 100 shares for sale at 180$\frac{1}{8}$, none at all at 180$\frac{1}{4}$, and only 500 at 180$\frac{3}{8}$. The jump from $\frac{1}{8}$ to $\frac{3}{8}$ emphasizes both the absence of pressure and persistency on the part of the buyers. They are not content to wait patiently until they can secure the stock at 180$\frac{1}{4}$; they reach for it, and, finding themselves clutching the air, are obliged to reach higher. The same thing on the opposite side shows lack of support.

**Jumps**

Each indication is to be judged not so much by rule as according to the conditions surrounding it. The tape furnishes a continuous series of motion pictures, with their respective explanations written between the printings. These are in a language which is foreign to all but Tape Readers, but anyone can learn a foreign language.

These volumes which we have been discussing are least liable to mislead when manipulation prevails, for the

**Effect of
Manipulation**

manipulator is obliged to deal in large blocks of stock, and must continually show his hand. A complete manipulative operation on the long side consists of three parts: Accumulation, marking up, and distribution. In the case of a short operation the distribution comes first, then the mark down and the accumulation. No one of these three sections is complete without the other two. (For full details see my series on Manipulations in Vols. 1 and 2 of THE TICKER.)

The manipulator must work with a large block of stock or the deal will not be worth his time, the risk and expenses. The Tape Reader must, therefore, be on the lookout for extensive operations on either side of the market. Accumulation will show itself in the quantities and in the way they appear on the tape. Having detected the accumulation, the Tape Reader has only to watch its progress, holding himself in readiness to take on some of the issue the moment the marking-up period begins. He does not buy it at once, because it may take weeks or months for the manipulator to complete his line; also, there might be opportunities to buy cheaper. Holding off until the psychological moment forces someone else to carry the stock for him—to pay his interest, so to speak. Furthermore, his capital is left free in the meantime.

When the marking up begins he gets in at the commencement of the move, and

## Volumes and Their Significance

goes along with it till there are signs of a halt or distribution. Having passed through the first two periods, he is in a position to fully benefit by the third stage of the operation. In this sort of work a figure chart, which I described in Vol I of THE TICKER, will help him, especially if the manipulative operation is continued over a considerable period— it will give him a bird's-eye view of the deal, enabling him to drop or resume the thread at any stage.

The Psychological Moment.

# VI. Market Technique

ON Saturday morning, February 27th, the market opened slightly higher than the previous night's close. Reading was the most active stock. After touching 123½ it slid off to 122½, at which point it invited short sales. This indication was emphasized at 122, at 121½ and again at 121. The downward trend was strongly marked until it struck 119⅞; then followed a quick rally of 1⅛ points.

This was a vicious three-point jab into a market which was only just recovering from the February break.

What was its effect on the other principal stocks? Union Pacific declined only ¾, Southern Pacific ⅝ and Steel ⅝. This proved that they were technically strong; that is, they were in hands which could view with equanimity a three-point break in a leading issue. Had this drive occurred when Reading was around 145 and Union 185 the effect upon the others would probably have been very different.

## Market Technique

In order to determine the extent of an ore body, miners use a diamond drill. This produces a core, the character of which shows what is beneath the surface. If it had been possible to have drilled into the market at the top of the recent rise, we should have found Floating Supply that the bulk of the floating supply in Steel, Reading and some others was held by a class of traders who buy heavily in booms and on bulges. These people operate with a comparatively small supply of margins, nerve and experience. They are exceedingly vulnerable, hence the stocks in which they operate suffer the greatest declines when the market receives a jar. The figures are interesting.

| | ——Points—— | | Per cent. |
| | 1907-9 Advance. | Feb'y, '09 Break. | of break to adv. |
|---|---|---|---|
| U. P. ... | 84⅞ | 12⅜ | 14.7 |
| Reading . | 73⅞ | 26⅜ | 33.6 |
| Steel ... | 36⅞ | 16½ | 44.6 |

The above shows that the public was heavily extended in Steel, somewhat less loaded with Reading, and was carrying very little Union Pacific. In other words, Union showed technical strength by its resistance to pressure, whereas Reading and Steel offered little or no opposition to the decline.

Both the market as a whole and individual stocks are to be judged as much by

# Tape Reading

A Three-point Break in Reading which had little effect upon the other leaders, proving the market technically strong

| Reading Co. | | | | | |
|---|---|---|---|---|---|
| | | 2100 | .....121¾ | 200 | .....120⅝ |
| 1700 | .....123 | 300 | .....121⅝ | 500 | .....120⅞ |
| 200 | .....123⅛ | 2000 | .....121½ | 1200 | .....121 |
| 500 | .....123 | 11 A. M. | | 200 | .....120⅞ |
| 500 | .....122⅞ | 1700 | .....121¼ | 100 | .....120¾ |
| 1300 | .....123 | 200 | .....121⅜ | 600 | .....120⅞ |
| 500 | .....123¼ | 600 | .....121¼ | 1000 | .....121 |
| 1900 | .....123¼ | 100 | .....121⅜ | 700 | .....121¼ |
| 1500 | .....123⅛ | 2700 | .....121¼ | 400 | .....121⅛ |
| 200 | .....123¼ | 100sld. | ...121⅛ | 900 | .....121¼ |
| 400 | .....123⅛ | 200 | .....121⅜ | 400 | .....121⅜ |
| 1100 | .....123 | 400 | .....121¼ | 700 | .....121¼ |
| 1200 | .....123⅛ | 1400 | .....121½ | 1000 | .....121⅛ |
| 300 | .....122⅞ | 200 | .....121⅜ | 600 | .....121 |
| 1500 | .....122¾ | 400 | .....121¼ | 1000 | .....121¼ |
| 1400 | .....122⅝ | 1100 | .....121 | 1100 | .....121⅜ |
| 1200 | .....122½ | 100 | .....120⅞ | 1000 | .....121¼ |
| 100 | .....122⅝ | 100 | .....121 | 200 | .....121⅜ |
| 3000 | .....122½ | 700 | .....120⅞ | 100 | .....121½ |
| 200 | .....122⅜ | 1400 | .....120⅝ | 200 | .....121⅝ |
| 700 | .....122½ | 700 | .....120½ | 300 | .....121⅜ |
| 100 | .....122⅝ | 700 | .....120⅝ | 1200 | .....121½ |
| 2000 | .....122⅜ | 1400 | .....120¾ | 500 | .....121⅝ |
| 500 | .....122½ | 100 | .....120⅝ | 1500 | .....121¾ |
| 200 | .....122⅜ | 900 | .....120½ | 1200 | .....121⅞ |
| 100 | .....122¼ | 2000 | .....120¼ | 500 | .....121¾ |
| 500 | .....122 | 100 | .....120⅜ | 200 | .....121⅝ |
| 100 | .....122⅛ | 500 | .....120¼ | 800 | .....121½ |
| 800 | .....122¼ | 500 | .....120⅜ | Un. Pac. Ry. | |
| 100 | .....122⅜ | 1500 | .....120½ | 1500 | .....177 |
| 100 | .....122½ | 800 | .....120⅜ | 500 | .....176⅞ |
| 600 | .....122⅜ | 600 | .....120¼ | 1900 | .....177 |
| 700 | .....122¼ | 400 | .....120⅜ | 700 | .....176⅞ |
| 1200 | .....122⅛ | 300 | .....120¼ | 700 | .....177 |
| 100 | .....122¼ | 800 | .....120⅛ | 600 | .....176⅞ |
| 100 | .....122⅛ | 200 | .....120⅜ | 500 | .....177 |
| 100 | .....122¼ | 100 | .....120½ | 1500 | .....177⅛ |
| 100 | .....122⅜ | 1300 | .....120⅜ | 1200 | .....177¼ |
| 2100 | .....122¼ | 1600 | .....120½ | 1200 | .....177⅜ |
| 400 | .....122 | 600 | .....120⅜ | 200 | .....177¼ |
| 300 | .....122⅛ | 700 | .....120¼ | 600 | .....177⅜ |
| 500 | .....122¼ | 2000 | .....120 | 300 | .....177¼ |
| 200 | .....122⅛ | 100 | .....120⅛ | 1100 | .....177⅜ |
| 1500 | .....122 | 1500 | .....120 | 900 | .....177½ |
| 200 | .....122⅛ | 100 | .....119⅞ | 2400 | .....177⅜ |
| 100 | .....122 | 200 | .....120 | 200 | .....177¼ |
| 1900 | .....122⅛ | 200 | .....120⅛ | 100 | .....177⅜ |
| 1600 | .....122 | 200 | .....120 | 700 | .....177¼ |
| 100 | .....122⅛ | 1000 | .....120⅛ | 500 | .....177⅜ |
| 500 | .....122 | 1700 | .....119⅞ | 1300 | .....177¼ |
| 100 | .....121⅞ | 200 | .....120 | 200 | .....177⅜ |
| 1500 | .....122 | 100 | .....119⅞ | 1200 | .....177¼ |
| 300 | .....121⅞ | 1600 | .....120 | 1700 | .....177⅜ |
| 500 | .....121¾ | 1100 | .....120¼ | 2000 | .....177¼ |
| 1500 | .....121¾ | 500 | .....120½ | 200 | .....177⅛ |

| | | | | | |
|---|---|---|---|---|---|
| 1200 | ......177¼ | 200 | ......117⅜ | 9100 | ......44⅝ |
| 300 | ......177⅜ | 100 | ......117½ | 2000 | ......44¾ |
| 100 | ......177½ | 1100 | ......117⅜ | 2700 | ......44⅝ |
| 300 | ......177⅜ | 200 | ......117¼ | 2500 | ......44¾ |
| 700 | ......177¼ | 300 | ......117⅜ | 400sld. | ...44½ |
| 1100 | ......177⅜ | 400 | ......117¼ | 600 | ......44¾ |
| 1600 | ......177½ | 200 | ......117⅛ | 700 | ......44⅝ |
| 300 | ......177⅜ | 100 | ......117¼ | 100 | ......44¾ |
| 900 | ......177¼ | 200 | ......117⅛ | 200 | ......44⅝ |
| 100 | ......177⅜ | 100 | ......117⅜ | 500 | ......44¾ |
| 100 | ......177¼ | 600 | ......117¼ | 100 | ......44⅝ |
| 600 | ......177⅛ | 20 | ......117⅜ | 2000 | ......44¾ |
| 1300 | ......177¼ | 600 | ......117⅜ | 900 | ......44⅝ |
| 700 | ......177⅛ | 100 | ......117¼ | 100 | ......44¾ |

11 A. M.

| | | | | | |
|---|---|---|---|---|---|
| | | 500 | ......117⅛ | 1400 | ......44⅝ |
| | | 200 | ......117 | 600 | ......44½ |
| 100 | ......177 | 100 | ......117⅛ | 1800 | ......44⅝ |
| 3900 | ......177⅛ | 400 | ......117 | 2600 | ......44½ |
| 1200 | ......177 | 300 | ......117⅛ | 500 | ......44⅝ |
| 1500 | ......176⅞ | 100 | ......117 | 100 | ......44½ |
| 200 | ......176¾ | | | 1700 | ......44⅝ |
| 1300 | ......176⅞ | 11 A. M. | | 1500 | ......44½ |
| 700 | ......177 | | | 900 | ......44⅝ |
| 100 | ......176⅞ | 300 | ......116⅞ | 1400 | ......44½ |
| 6300 | ......176¾ | 400 | ......117 | 1600 | ......44¾ |
| 1100 | ......176⅞ | 500 | ......116⅞ | 2100 | ......44¼ |
| 200 | ......177 | 400 | ......117 | | |
| 1400 | ......176⅞ | 100 | ......116⅞ | 11 A. M. | |
| 1600 | ......177 | 100 | ......116¾ | | |
| 100 | ......176⅞ | 1400 | ......116⅞ | 5600 | ......44¼ |
| 1300 | ......177 | 100 | ......116¾ | 500sld. | ...44⅜ |
| 200 | ......177⅛ | 100 | ......116⅞ | 1900 | ......44¼ |
| 200 | ......177 | 100 | ......116¾ | 200 | ......44⅛ |
| 1900 | ......177⅛ | 900 | ......116¾ | 700 | ......44¼ |
| 500 | ......177¼ | 700 | ......116⅞ | 100 | ......44⅛ |
| 1400 | ......177⅛ | 200 | ......116¾ | 1200 | ......44¼ |
| Southern Pac. | | 400 | ......116⅞ | 1100 | ......44⅛ |
| 500 | ......117¼ | 400 | ......117 | 2500 | ......44¼ |
| 400 | ......117¼ | U. S. Steel | | 2500 | ......44⅛ |
| 200 | ......117¼ | | | 5000 | ......44¼ |
| 1800 | ......117⅜ | 3000 | ....{ 44½ | 3200 | ......44⅜ |
| 400 | ......117¼ | | { 44⅝ | 500 | ......44½ |
| | | | | 100 | ......44⅜ |

what they do as what they do not do at critical points. If the big fellows who accumulated Union below 120 had distributed it above 180, the stock would have broken something like thirty **Technical** points, owing to its having passed from **Conditions** strong to weak hands. As it did not have any such decline, but only a very small reaction, compared to its advance, the Tape Reader infers that Union is destined for much higher prices; that it offers comparative immunity from declines and a possible large advance in the near future.

This should not be taken as a prediction. Even were Union Pacific scheduled for a thirty-point rise in the next two weeks, something might happen to-morrow to postpone the campaign for a considerable time. But the Tape Reader must work with these broader considerations in full view. He has just so much time and capital and this must be employed where it will yield the greatest results. If by watching for the most favorable opportunities he can operate with the trend in a stock which will some day or week show him ten points profit over any other issue he could have chosen, he is increasing his chances to that extent.

A long advance or decline usually culminates in a wide, quick movement in the leaders. Take the break of February 23d last: Reading declined from 128¾ to 118 and Steel from 46 to 41¼ in one day. Southern Pacific, after creeping up last fall from 97 to 112, reached a climax in a seven-point jump during one session. Instances are so numerous that they are hardly worth citing. The same thing happens in the market as a whole—an exceptionally violent movement, after a protracted sag or rise, usually indicates its culmination.

Culminations

A stock generally shows the Tape Reader what it proposes to do by its action under pressure or stimulation. For example: On Friday, February 19th, 1909, the United States Steel Corporation announced an open market in steel products. The news was out. Everybody in the country knew it by the following morning. The Tape Reader, in weighing the situation before the next day's opening, would reason: "As the news is public property, the normal thing for Steel and the market to do is to rally. Steel closed last night at 48⅜. The market hinges upon this one stock. Let's see how it acts."

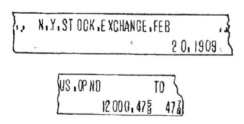

This is ¾ down from last night's closing—a perfectly natural occurrence in view of yesterday's announcement. The real test of strength or weakness will follow. For the first ten minutes Steel comes

---

200 . 47⅞ . 4500 . ¾ . 1200 . ⅞ . 1500 . ¾

---

without otherwise varying.

Eighteen times the price swings back and forth between the same fractions. Meantime, Union Pacific, which opened at 177½, shows a tendency to rally and pull the rest of the market up behind it.

12 00 , 178 , 200 , ⅛ , 400 , ¼ , 200 , 178¼ , 700 , ⅜

**An Interesting Contest**

Can Union lift Steel? That is the question. Here are two opposing forces, and the Tape Reader watches like a hawk, for he is going with the market— in the direction of the trend. Union is up ⅞ from the opening and Southern Pacific is reinforcing it.

U         AR    SP
500 , 178⅜   84⅝  118⅜      500 , ½

But Steel does not respond. Not once does it get out of that ¾-⅞ rut—not even a single hundred shares sells at 48. This proves that it is freely offered at 47⅞ and that it possesses no rallying

power, in spite of the leadership displayed by the Harrimans.

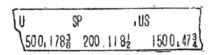

Union makes a final effort to induce a
following,

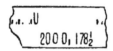

to which Steel replies by breaking
through with a thud.

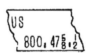

This is the Tape Reader's cue to go **The Signal**
short. In an instant he has put out a
line of Steel for which he gets $47\frac{1}{2}$ or
$47\frac{3}{8}$, as there are large volumes traded
in at those figures.

Union Pacific is disheartened. The
Steel millstone is hanging round its neck.
It slides off to $178\frac{3}{4}$ . $\frac{1}{4}$ . $\frac{1}{8}$ and
finally to

The pressure on Steel increases at the low level.

| US | NP | US |
|---|---|---|
| 3500. 47½ | 4S,1,103½ | 47⅜ |

Successive sales are made, as follows:

6800 . 47½ . 2600 . ⅜ . 500¼ . 8800 . ⅛

**Liquidation**

From this time on there is a steady flow of long stock. Reading and Pennsylvania are the weakest railroads. Colorado Fuel breaks 7 points in a running decline and the other steel stocks follow suit. U. S. Steel is dumped in bunches at the bid prices, and even the dignified preferred is sympathetically affected.

| US | | PR | | |
|---|---|---|---|---|
| 500,46⅝ | ,3500,½ | 200,110¼ | ,200,⅛ | ,1600,110 |

The market closes at the bottom, with Steel at 46, leaving thousands of stockholders of Steel in a thoroughly frightened state, their accounts weakened by the decline and a holiday ahead for them to worry over.

It looks to the Tape Reader as though the stock would go lower on the following Tuesday. At any rate, no covering indication has appeared, and unless it is his invariable rule to close every trade each day, he puts a stop at 47 on his short Steel and goes his way. (His original stop was 48⅛.)

Steel opens on the following session at 44¾@½, and during the day makes 41¼.

There are a number of lessons to be drawn from this episode. The market is a tug-o'-war. Successful tape reading requires ability to judge which side has the greatest pulling power and one must have the courage to go with that side. There are critical points which occur in each swing, just as in the life of a business or of an individual. At these junctures it seems as though a feather's weight on either side would determine the immediate trend. Any one who can spot these points has everything to win and little to lose, for he can always play with a stop placed close behind the turning point or point of resistance.

*Critical Points*

If Union had continued in its upward course, gaining in power, volume and influence as it progressed, the dire effects of the Steel situation might have been overcome. It was simply a question of pulling power, and Steel pulled Union down.

This study of responses is one of the most valuable in the Tape Reader's education. It is an almost unerring guide to the technical position of the market. Of course, all responses are not clearly defined. It is a matter of indifference to the Tape Reader as to who or what produces these tests, or critical periods. They constantly appear and disappear;

*Responses*

he must make his diagnosis and act accordingly. If a stock is being manipulated higher, the movement will seldom be continued unless other stocks follow and support the advance. If the public is in control of a stock, the other issues should be watched to see whether large operators are unloading on the strong spots. Should a stock fail to break on bad news. it means that insiders have anticipated the decline and stand ready to buy.

A member of a syndicate once said to me:

"We are going to dissolve to-morrow."

"Will there not be considerable selling by people who don't want to carry their share of the securities?" I asked.

"Well," he replied, "we know how every one stands. Probably 10,000 shares will come on the market from a few members who are obliged to sell, and as a few of us have sold that much short in anticipation, we'll be there to buy it when the time comes."

**The Turn in Rock Island** This reminds us that it is well to consider the insider's probable attitude on a stock. The tape usually indicates what this is. One of the muckraking magazines recently showed that Rock Island preferred had been driven down to 28 last August, to the accompaniment of receivership rumors. The writer of the article was unable to prove that these rumors originated with the insiders, but states that the transactions at this time were inscrutable. Perhaps they were inscrutable to a person inexperienced in tape reading, but we well remember that the indications were all in favor of buying the stock; the transactions were very large—out of all proportion to the capital stock outstanding and the floating supply. What did this mean to the Tape Reader? Thousands of shares of stock were traded in per day, after a ten-point decline and a small rally. If the volume of sales represented long stock, some one was there to buy it. If there was manipulation it certainly was not for the purpose of distributing the stock at such a low level. So, by casting out the unlikely factors, we arrived at the correct conclusion. We state this advisedly, because we stood at the ticker and reasoned the situation out at the time.

The market is being put to the test continually by one element of which little has been said, viz., the floor traders. These shrewd fellows are always on the alert to ferret out a weak spot in the market, for they love the short side. Lack of support, if detected, in an issue generally leads to a raid which if the technical situation is weak spreads to other parts of the floor and produces a reaction or a slump all around. Or, if they find a vulnerable short interest, they are quick to bid

Floor Traders

up a stock and drive the shorts to cover. With these and other operations going on all the time, the Tape Reader who is at all expert is seldom at a loss to know on which side his best chances lie. Other people are doing for him what he would do himself if he were all-powerful.

**The Broad Movements**

While it is the smaller swings that interest him most, the Tape Reader must not fail to keep his bearings in relation to the broader movements of the market. When a panic prevails he recognizes in it the birth of a bull market and operates with the certainty that prices will gradually rise until a boom marks the other extreme of the swing. In a bull market he considers reactions of from two to five points normal and reasonable; he looks for occasional drops of 10 to 15 points in the leaders, with a 25-point break at least once a year. When any of these occur, he knows what to look for next.

In a bull market he expects a drop of 10 points to be followed by a recovery of at least half the decline, and if the rise is to continue, all of the drop and more will be recovered. If a stock or the market refuses to rally naturally, he knows that the trouble has not been overcome, and therefore looks for a further decline.

Take American Smelters, which made a top at 99⅝ last November, then slumped off under rumors of competition until it reached 78. Covering indications appeared around 79½. Had the operator also gone long here, he could confidently have expected Smelters to rally to 88¾. The decline having been 21⅝ points, there was a rally of 10¾ points due. As a matter of record the stock did recover to 89⅜.

Of course, these things are mere guide posts, as the Tape Reader's actual trading is done only on the most positive and promising indications; but they are valuable in teaching him what to avoid. For instance, he would be wary about making an initial short sale of Smelters after a 15-point break, even if his indications were clear. There might be several points more on the short side, but he would realize that every point further decline would bring him closer to the turning point, and after such a violent break the safest money was on the long side.

**Guide Posts**

Another instance: Reading sold on January 4th, 1909, at 144⅜. By the end of the month it touched 131½, and on February 23d broke ten points to 118. This was a decline of 24⅜ points, allowing for the 2 per cent. dividend. As previously stated, the stock looked like an attractive short sale, not only on the first breakdown, but on the final drive. The conservative trader would have waited for a buying indication, as there would have been less risk on the long side. The element of safety is as important as any other.

It is seldom that the market runs more than three or four consecutive days in one direction without a reaction, hence the Tape Reader must realize that his chances decrease as the swing is prolonged.

The daily movements offer his best opportunities; but he must keep in stocks which swing wide enough to enable him to grab a profit.

**An Hourly Cycle**

It is an astonishing fact, and one which we have never before seen in print, that there is a market cycle which runs almost exactly one hour.

Watch it for yourself when next at the ticker, and you will find that if an upward movement culminates at 10:25 the reaction usually will last till 10:55, and the apex of the next up swing will occur about thirty minutes later. I have actually stood watch in hand, having decided what to do, waiting for the high or low moment on which to sell or buy, and have often hit within a fraction of the best obtainable figure. Why this is I do not attempt to explain, but it happens very often.

I have frequently used this idea as a test of the market's strength or weakness, in this way: If a decline ended at a certain moment and the subsequent rally only lasted ten minutes, instead of the normal half hour, I would consider it an indication of weakness and would look for a further decline.

This is valuable more as a check on over-anxiety to act, as it gives a definite point at which commitments may be made to greatest advantage. As Napoleon said: "The adroit man profits by everything, neglects nothing which may increase his chances."

**Napoleon's Maxim**

I once knew a speculator who bought and sold by the clock. He had no idea of the hourly swing, but would buy at 12 o'clock, because it was 12 o'clock, and would sell at 2 o'clock, for the same reason.

The methods employed by the average outside speculator are not so very much of an improvement on this, which explains why so many lose their money.

The expert Tape Reader is diametrically opposed to such people and their methods.

He applies science and skill in his angling for profits.

**Science and Skill**

He studies, figures, analyzes and deduces. He knows exactly where he stands, what he is doing and why.

Few people are willing to go to the very bottom of things. Is it any wonder that success is for the few?

## VII. Dull Markets and Their Opportunities

MANY people are apt to regard a dull market as a calamity. They claim: "Our hands are tied; we can't get out of what we've got; if we could there'd be no use getting in again, for whatever we do we can't make a dollar."

Tape Sitters Such people are not Tape Readers. They are Sitters. They are Billikens ex-grin.

As a matter of fact, dull markets offer innumerable opportunities and we have only to dig beneath the crust of prejudice to find them.

Dulness in the market or in any special stock means that the forces capable of influencing it in either an upward or a downward direction have temporarily come to a balance. The best illustration is that of a clock which is about run down—its pendulum gradually decreases the width of its swings until it comes to a complete standstill, thus:

How the market pendulum comes to a standstill

Now turn this on its side and you see what the chart of a stock or the market looks like when it reaches the point of dulness.

These dull periods occur most frequently after a season of delirious activity on the bull side. People make money, pyramid on their profits and glut themselves with stocks at the top. As every one is loaded up, there is comparatively no one left to buy, and the break which inevitably follows would happen if there were no bears, no bad news or anything else to force a decline.

Nature has her own remedy for dissipation. She presents the débauché with a thumping head and a moquette tongue. These tend to keep him quiet until the damage can be repaired.

**Nature's Remedy**

So with these intervals of market rest. Traders who have placed themselves in a position to be trimmed are duly trimmed. They lose their money and (temporarily) their nerve. The market, therefore, becomes neglected. Extreme dulness sets in.

If the history of the market were to be written, these periods of lifelessness should mark the close of each chapter. The reason is: The factors which were active in producing the main movement, with its start, its climax and its collapse, have spent their force. Prices, therefore, settle into a groove, where they remain sometimes for weeks or until affected by some other powerful influence.

When a market is in the midst of a big move, no one can tell how long or how far it will run. But when prices are stationary, we know that *from this point* there will be a pronounced swing in one direction or another.

**The Next Swing**

There are ways of anticipating the direction of this swing. One is by noting the technical strength or weakness of the market, as described in a previous chapter. The resistance to pressure mentioned as characteristic of the dull period in March, 1909, has been followed by a pronounced rise, and at this writing the leading stocks are many points higher. This is particularly true of Reading, in which the shakeouts around 120 (one of which was described) were frequent and positive. When insiders shake other people out it means that they want the stock themselves. These are good times for us to get in, for then we will enjoy having Mr. Frick and his friends work for *us*.

### Dull Markets and Their Opportunities

When a dull market shows its inability to hold rallies, or when it does not respond to bullish news, it is technically weak, and unless something comes along to change the situation, the next swing will be downward.

On the other hand, when there is a gradual hardening in prices; when bear raids fail to dislodge considerable quantities of stock; when stocks do not decline upon unfavorable news, we may look for an advancing market in the near future.

No one can tell when a dull market **Watch a Dull** will merge into a very active one; there- **Market** fore the Tape Reader must be constantly on the watch. It is foolish for him to say: "The market is dead dull. No use going downtown to-day. The leaders only swung less than a point yesterday. Nothing in such a market."

Such reasoning is apt to make one miss the very choicest opportunities, viz., those of getting in on the ground floor of a big move. For example: During the aforesaid accumulation in Reading, the stock ranged between 120 and 124½. Without warning, it one day gave indication (around 125) that the absorption was about concluded, and the stock had begun its advance. The Tape Reader, having reasoned beforehand that this accumulation was no piker's game, would have grabbed a bunch of Reading as soon as the indication appeared. He might have bought more than he wanted for scalping purposes, with the intention of holding part of his line for a long swing, using the rest for regular trading.

As the stock drew away from his purchase price he could have raised his stop on the lot he intended to hold, putting a mental label on it to the effect that it is to be sold when he detects inside distribution. Thus he stands to benefit to the fullest extent by any manipulative work which may be done. In other words, he says: "I'll get out of this lot when Mr. Frick and his friends get out of theirs."

**Accumulation**

He feels easy in his mind about this stock, because he has seen the accumulation and knows it has relieved the market of all the floating supply at about this level.

This means a sharp, quick rise sooner or later, as little stock is to be met with on the way up. If he neglected to watch the market continuously and get in at the very start, his chances would be greatly lessened. He might not have the courage to take on the larger quantity.

On Friday, March 26, 1909, Reading and Union were about as dull as two gentlemanly leaders could well be. Reading opened at 132¾, high was 133¼, low 132¼, last 132⅝. Union's extreme fluctuation was ⅝—from 180⅝ to 181¼. Activity was confined to such "pups" as Beet Sugar, Mexican Central and Kansas City Southern.

The following day, Saturday, the opening gave every indication that the previous day's dulness would be repeated, initial sales showing only fractional changes. Copper, B. & O., Wabash pfd. and MOP were up ⅜ or½. Union was ⅛ higher and Reading ⅛ lower. Beet Sugar was down ⅝, with sales at 32.

Reading showed 1100 . 132½ . 800 . ⅜, Union 800 . 181 . 400 . 181 . 200 . ⅛ . 400 . 181. A single hundred Steel at 45⅛. B. & O. 109⅞ . ¾. Reading 132½. Beet Sugar 31¾ . 400 . ⅞. Union 800 . 180⅞. Steel 1000 . 45. Beet 800 . 32. Steel 1500 . 45. Reading 132⅝. Steel 44⅞. Market dead. Mostly 100-share lots.

Reading 1600 . 132½. Steel 400 . 45. Beet Sugar looks good on the bull side, 300 . 32¼ . 700 . ⅜. Union 200 . 180⅞. Reading 500 . 132⅜. Union 300 . 180¾.

10.15 A. M.—American Sugar now responds slightly to the strength in Beet Sugar, but we should rather not see the cart before the horse. Sugar 200 . 130⅞ . 600 . 131. Beet 32½ . 600 . ⅝. This stock holds the spot-light. Others inanimate.

Ah! Here's our cue! Reading 2300 **The Cue** . 132½ . 2000 . ½ . 500 . ⅝. Coming out of a dead market, quantities like these taken at the offered prices can mean only one thing, and without quibbling the Tape Reader takes on a bunch of Reading "at the market."

Whatever is doing in Reading, the rest of the market is slow to respond, although N. Y. Central seems willing to help a little—500 . 127½ (after ¼). Beets are up to 33¼. Steel is 45⅛, and Copper 71¼—a fraction better.

Reading 300 . 132½. Steel 1300 . 45⅛ . ¼. Union 181. Reading 300 . 132⅝. Beets 33½. Union 700 . 181⅛. N. Y. Central 127⅝ . 600 . ¾ . ⅞. There's some assistance!

Union 900 . 181⅛. Reading 132¾. Copper 700 . 71½. Reading 800 . 132⅞ . 133 . 900 . 133 . 1100 . ⅛. Central 300 . 127¾. Union 400 . 181⅛ . 300 . ¼. Reading 1500 . 133¼ . 3500 . ½. Not much doubt about the trend now. The whole market is responding to Reading, and there is a steady increase in power, breadth and volume. The rapid advances show that short covering is no small factor. Union 400 . 181⅜ . 700 . ½ . 400 . ⅝.

**Getting Into Active Stocks**

It looks as though a lot of people are throwing their Beet Sugar and getting into the big stocks. St. Paul, Copper and American Smelters begin to lift a little.

Around 11 A. M. there is a brief period of hesitation, in which the market seems to take a long breath in preparation for another effort. There is scarcely any reaction and no weakness. Reading backs up a fraction to 133 ¼ and Union to 181⅜. There are no selling indications, so the Tape Reader stands by his guns.

Now they are picking up again— Reading 133⅜ . ½ . ⅝ . ¾. Union

181⅝. Central 128⅛ . 700 . ¼. Atchison 1000 . 104½ . 600 . ⅝. Northern Pacific is complaisant, 141½ . ⅝. Union 1000 . 181½ . 3500 . ⅝ . 2800 . ¾ . 2800 . ⅞ . 4100 . 182. Steel 45½. Southern Pacific 121. St. Paul 146. Reading 2100 . 133⅞ . 1100 . 134 . 1700 . ⅛.

From then right up to the close it's nothing but bull, and everything closes within a fraction of its highest. Reading makes 134⅜, Union 183, Steel 46⅛, Central 128⅞, and the rest in proportion. The market has gained such headway that it will take dire news to prevent a high, wide opening on Monday, and the Tape Reader has his choice of closing out at the high point or putting in a stop and taking his chances over Sunday.

So we see the advantage of watching a dull market and getting in the moment it starts out of its rut. One could almost draw lines on the chart of a leader like Union or Reading (the upper line being the high point of its monotonous swing and the lower line the low point) and buy or sell whenever the line is crossed. For when a stock shakes itself loose from a narrow radius it is clear that the accumulation or distribution or resting spell has been completed and new forces are at work. These forces are most pronounced and effective at the beginning of the new move—more power is need-

**Breaking Over the Line**

ed to start a thing rolling than to keep it going.

Some of my readers may think I am giving illustrations after these things happen on the tape, and that what a Tape Reader *would have done* at the time is problematical. I therefore wish to state that my tape illustrations are taken from the indications which actually showed themselves when they were freshly printed on the tape, at which time I did not know what was *going* to happen.

**Points of Resistance**

There are other ways in which a trader may employ himself during dull periods. One is to keep tab on the points of resistance in the leaders and play on them for fractional profits. This, we admit, is a rather precarious occupation, as the operating expenses constitute an extremely heavy percentage against the player, especially when the leading stocks only swing a point or so per day.

But if one chooses to take these chances rather than be idle, the best way is to keep a chart on which should be recorded every ⅛ fluctuation. This forms a picture of what is occurring and clearly defines the points of resistance, as well as the momentary trend. In the following chart the stock opens at 181¼ and the first point of resistance is 181½. The first indication of a downward trend is shown in the dip to 181⅛, and with these two straws showing the tendency, the Tape Reader goes short "at the market," getting, say, 181⅛ (we'll give ourselves the worst of it).

After making one more unsuccessful attempt to break through the resistance at 181½, the trend turns unmis-

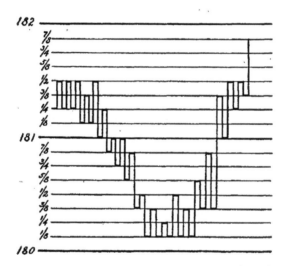

Chart showing points of resistance in a dull market

takably downward, as shown by an almost unbroken series of lower tops and bottoms. These indicate that the pressure is heavy enough to force the price to new low levels, and at the same time it is sufficient to prevent the rally going quite as high as on the previous bulge.

At 180⅛ a new point of resistance appears. The decline is checked. The

**Tops and Bottoms**

Tape Reader must cover and go long. The steps are now upward and as the price approaches the former point of resistance he watches it narrowly for his indication to close out. This time, however, there is but slight opposition to the advance, and the price breaks through. He keeps his long stock.

**A Double Stop**

In making the initial trade he placed a "double" stop at 181⅝ or ¾, on the ground that if his stock overcame the resistance at 181½ it would go higher and he would have to go with it. Being short 100 shares, his double stop order would read: "Buy 200 at 181⅝ stop." Of course the price might just catch his stop and go lower. These things will happen, and anyone who cannot face them without becoming perturbed had better learn self control.

After going long around the low point, he should place another double stop at 180 or 179⅞, for if the point of resistance is broken through after he has covered and gone long, he must switch his position in an instant. Not to do so would place him in the attitude of a guesser. If he is playing on this plan he must not dilute it with other ideas.

Remember this method is only applicable to a very dull market, and, as we have said, is precarious business. We cannot recommend it. It will not as a rule pay the Tape Reader to attempt scalping fractions out of the leaders in a dull market. Commissions, tax stamps and the invisible eighth, in addition to frequent losses, form too great a handicap. There must be wide swings if profits are to exceed losses, and the thing to do is, wait for good opportunities. "The market is always with us" is an old and a true saying. We are not compelled to trade and results do not depend on *how often* we trade, but on *how much money* we make.

There is another way of turning a dull market to good account, and that is by trading in the stocks which are temporarily active, owing to manipulative or other causes. The Tape Reader does not care a picayune what sort of a label they put on the goods. Call a stock "Harlem Goats preferred" if you like, and make it active, preferably by means of manipulation, and the agile Tape Reader will trade in it with profit. It matters not to him whether it's a railroad or a shooting gallery; whether it declares regular or "Irish" dividends; whether the abbreviation is X Y Z or Z Y X—so long as it furnishes indications and a broad market on which to get in and out.

**Trading in the Specialties**

Take Beet Sugar on March 26, 1909, the day on which Union and Reading were so dull. It was a pipe to beat Beet Sugar. Even an embryo Tape Reader would have gone long at 30 or below, and as it never left him in doubt he could have dumped it at the top just before the close, or held it till next day, when it touched 33½.

## American Beet Sugar

An Example

| | | |
|---|---|---|
| 700 . . . . . 29¼ | 100 . . . . . 30½ | |
| 200 . . . . . 29⅜ | 100 . . . . . 30⅜ | |
| 900 . . . . . 29¼ | 600 . . . . . 30½ | |
| 500 . . . . . 29⅜ | 500 . . . . . 30⅜ | |
| 700 . . . . . 29½ | 500 . . . . . 30½ | |
| 200 . . . . . 29⅝ | 100 . . . . . 30⅜ | |
| 900 . . . . . 29¾ | 100 . . . . . 30¼ | |
| 1100 . . . . . 29⅞ | 100 . . . . . 30⅜ | |
| 1000 . . . . . 30 | **12 M.** | |
| 500 . . . . . 30⅛ | 200 . . . . . 30⅜ | |
| 100 . . . . . 30¼ | 700 . . . . . 30⅛ | |
| 100 . . . . . 30⅜ | 100 . . . . . 30⅝ | |
| 100 . . . . . 30¼ | | |
| 600 . . . . . 30⅜ | **1 P. M.** | |
| 1100 . . . . . 30½ | 200 . . . . . 30¾ | |
| 400 . . . . . 30⅜ | 100 . . . . . 32⅝ | |
| 100 . . . . . 30¼ | 500 . . . . . 30½ | |
| 700 . . . . . 30⅜ | 200 . . . . . 30⅝ | |
| 100 . . . . . 30½ | 1000 . . . . . 30¾ | |
| 200 . . . . . 30⅜ | 700 . . . . . 30⅞ | |
| 1300 . . . . . 30¼ | 600 . . . . . 31 | |
| 200 . . . . . 30⅜ | 600 . . . . . 31⅛ | |
| 300 . . . . . 30½ | 300 . . . . . 31¼ | |
| 400 . . . . . 30⅝ | 200 . . . . . 31⅜ | |
| 100 . . . . . 30¾ | 100 . . . . . 31¼ | |
| 100 . . . . . 30⅝ | 400 . . . . . 31⅜ | |
| 100 . . . . . 30½ | 400 . . . . . 31½ | |
| 100 . . . . . 30⅝ | 100 . . . . . 31⅝ | |
| 600 . . . . . 30½ | 200 . . . . . 31⅜ | |
| 100 . . . . . 30⅝ | 200 . . . . . 31½ | |
| 400 . . . . . 30½ | 300 . . . . . 31⅝ | |
| **11 A. M.** | 200 . . . . . 31½ | |
| 200 . . . . . 30½ | 200 . . . . . 31⅝ | |
| 400 . . . . . 30⅝ | 200 . . . . . 31½ | |
| 900 . . . . . 30¾ | 300 . . . . . 31⅝ | |
| 100 . . . . . 30⅝ | **2 P. M.** | |
| 200 . . . . . 30½ | 100 . . . . . 31⅝ | |
| 200 . . . . . 30⅜ | 700 . . . . . 31¾ | |

| | | | | |
|---|---|---|---|---|
| 700 | . . . . . | 31⅞ | 300 . . . . . . | 32⅛ |
| 400 | . . . . . | 32 | 400 . . . . . | 32¼ |
| 600 | . . . . . . | 32¼ | 800 . . . . . | 32⅜ |
| 600 | . . . . . | 32⅛ | 1000 . . . . . | 32½ |
| 900 | . . . . . | 32¼ | 200 . . . . . . | 32⅝ |

On March 5, 1909, Kansas City Southern spent the morning drifting between 42¾ and 43½. Shortly after the noon hour the stock burst into activity and large volume. Does any sane person suppose that a hundred or more people became convinced that Kansas City Southern was a purchase at that particular moment? What probably started the rise was the placing of manipulative orders, in which purchases predominated. Thus the sudden activity, the volume and the advancing tendency gave notice to the Tape Reader to "get aboard." The manipulator showed his hand and the **"Get Aboard"** Tape Reader had only to go along with the current.

### Kansas City Southern

| | | | | |
|---|---|---|---|---|
| 500 | . . . . . | 43⅜ | 100 . . . . . . | 43⅛ |
| 100 | . . . . . | 43½ | 200 . . . . . | 43 |
| 10 | . . . . . | 43½ | 400 . . . . . | 42⅞ |
| 200 | . . . . . | 43⅜ | 300 . . . . . | 43¾ |
| 200 | . . . . : | 43½ | 100 . . . . . | 43 |
| 100 | . . . . . | 43⅜ | | |
| 100 | . . . . . | 43½ | 11 A. M. | |
| 100 | . . . . . | 43¼ | 200 . . . . . | 43 |
| 200 | . . . . . | 43⅛ | 100 . . . . . | 42⅞ |
| 500 | . . . . . | 43 | 600 . . . . . | 43 |
| 200 | . . . . . | 43⅛ | 25 . . . . . | 43¼ |
| 500 | . . . . . | 43¼ | 100 . . . . . | 43¼ |
| 400 | . . . . . | 43⅛ | 100 . . . . . | 43⅜ |
| 100 | . . . . . | 43¼ | 100 . . . . . | 43¼ |

Tape Reading

| | | | | |
|---|---|---|---|---|
| 300 | . . . . . 43⅛ | 900 | . . . . . . 44⅞ |
| 500 | . . . . . 43¼ | 500 | . . . . . . 45 |
| 100 | . . . . . 43⅜ | 1800 | . . . . . . 44⅞ |
| 400 | . . . . . 43¼ | 300 | . . . . . . 44⅝ |
| 200 | . . . . . 43⅛ | | |

12 M.

2 P. M.

| | | | |
|---|---|---|---|
| 100 | . . . . . 43⅜ | 200 | . . . . . 44½ |
| 500 | . . . . . 43½ | 100 | . . . . . 44⅜ |
| 100 | . . . . . 43⅝ | 1000 | . . . . . 44½ |
| 400 | . . . . . 43½ | 300 | . . . . . 44⅝ |
| 200 | . . . . . 43⅝ | 600 | . . . . . 44¾ |
| 1200 | . . . . . 43¾ | 100 | . . . . . 44⅝ |
| 400 | . . . . . 43⅞ | 500 | . . . . . 44¾ |
| 2300 | . . . . . 44 | 1200 | . . . . . 44⅞ |
| 1300 | . . . . . 44⅛ | 200 | . . . . . 45 |
| 1400 | . . . . . 44¼ | 100 | . . . . . 44⅞ |
| 400 | . . . . . 44⅜ | 1500 | . . . . . 45 |
| 1500 | . . . . . 44¼ | 700 | . . . . 45⅛ |
| 100 | . . . . . 44⅛ | 400 | . . . . . 45¼ |
| 400 | . . . . . 44 | 700 | . . . . . 45⅛ |
| 1800 | . . . . . 44⅛ | 700 | . . . . . 45¼ |
| 200 | . . . . . 44 | 300 | . . . . 45⅜ |
| 800 | . . . . . 44⅛ | 100 | . . . . . 45¼ |
| 400 | . . . . . 44¼ | 400 | . . . . . 45⅜ |
| | | 900 | . . . . 45½ |

1 P. M.

| | | | |
|---|---|---|---|
| | | 100 | . . . . . 45⅝ |
| 200 | . . . . . 44¼ | 700 | . . . . . 45¾ |
| 800 | . . . . . 44⅜ | 700 | . . . . . 45⅞ |
| 100 | . . . . . 44¼ | 200 | . . . . . 45¾ |
| 300 | . . . . . 44⅜ | 900 | . . . . . 45⅞ |
| 600 | . . . . . 44½ | 1600 | . . . . . 46 |
| 100 | . . . . . 44⅜ | 1400 | . . . . . 46⅛ |
| 600 | . . . . . 44½ | 1000 | . . . . . 46⅜ |
| 800 | . . . . . 44⅝ | 1300 | . . . . . 46½ |
| 200 | . . . . . 44¾ | 500 | . . . . . 46⅝ |
| 300 | . . . . . 44⅝ | 200 | . . . . . 46¾ |
| 200 | . . . . . 44¾ | 500 | . . . . . 46⅝ |
| 300 | . . . . . 44⅝ | 1700 | . . . . . 46¾ |
| 700 | . . . . . 44¾ | 300 | . . . . . 46¾ |

**Pyramiding**

The advance was not only sustained, but emphasized at certain points. Here the Tape Reader could have pyramided, using a stop close behind his average cost and raising it so as to conserve profits. If he bought his first lot at 44, his second at 45, and his third at 46, he could have thrown the whole at 46⅝ and netted $406.50 for the day if he were trading in 100-share units, or $2,032.50 if trading in 500-share units.

## VIII. The Use of Charts as Guides and Indicators

**M**ANY interesting queries have been received by THE TICKER relating to the use of charts. The following is a representative communication:

**Figure Charts**

"Referring to your figure chart ex-
"plained in Volume I, I have found
"it a most valuable aid to detecting
"accumulation or distribution in
"market movements. I have been
"in Wall Street a number of years,
"and like many others have always
"shown a skeptical attitude toward
"charts and other mechanical meth-
"ods of forecasting trends; but after
"a thorough trial of the chart on
"Union Pacific, I find that I could
"have made a very considerable sum
"if I had followed the indications
"shown. I note your suggestions to
"operators to study earnings, etc.,
"and not to rely on charts, as they
"are very often likely to mislead. I
"regret that I cannot agree with
"you. You have often stated that
"the tape tells the story; since this
"is true, and a chart is but a copy
"of the tape, with indications of ac-

"cumulation or distribution, as the
"case may be, why not follow the
"chart entirely, and eliminate all un-
"necessary time devoted to study of
"earnings, etc.?"

Let us consider those portions of
the above which relate to Tape Reading, first clearly defining the difference
between chart operations and tape
reading.

The genuine chart player usually
operates in one stock at a time, using
as a basis the past movements of that
stock and following a more or less
definite code of rules. He treats the
market and his stock as a machine. He
uses no judgment as to market conditions, and does not consider the
movements of other stocks; but he ex-
ercises great discretion as to whether
he shall "play" an indication or not.

*The Chart Player*

The Tape Reader operates on what
the tape shows *now*. He is not wedded
to any particular issue, and, if he
chooses, can work without pencil, paper or memoranda of any sort. He
also has his code of rules—less clearly
defined than those of the chart player.
So many different situations present
themselves that his rules gradually become intuitive—a sort of second nature is evolved by self-training and experience.

A friend to whom I have given some
points in Tape Reading once asked if
I had my rules all down so fine that

I knew just which to use at certain
moments. I answered him thus:
When you cross a street where the
traffic is heavy, do you stop to consult
a set of rules showing when to run
ahead of a trolley car or when not to
dodge a wagon? No. You take a
look both ways and at the proper moment you walk across. Your mind may
be on something else or you may be
reading your newspaper while cross-
ing—your judgment tells you when to
start and how fast to walk. That is
the attitude of the trained Tape Reader.

The difference between the Chart
Player and the Tape Reader is therefore about as wide as between day and
night. We do not see how the chart
follower could mix Tape Reading with
his art without making a hodge-podge
of it. But there are ways in which
the Tape Reader may utilize charts as
guides and indicators and for the purpose of reinforcing his memory.

**Detecting Accumulation and Distribution**

First, as our correspondent says, the
Figure Chart (see TICKER, Vol. I, No.
4) is unquestionably the best mechanical means of detecting accumulation
and distribution. It is also valuable in
showing the main points of resistance
on the big swings.

A figure chart cannot be made from
the open, high, low and last prices,
such as are printed in the average
newspaper. We recall but three pub-

lications from which such charts may be constructed; viz., the official N. Y. Stock Exchange list, published by F. E. Fitch, 47 Broad St., N. Y.; the N. Y. *Evening Sun,* and the *Wall Street Journal.* For general accuracy, reliability and economy, we prefer the Evening *Sun,* which costs, postpaid, only 20 cents a month, or $2 a year.

Figure Chart of Amalgamated Copper During the 1903 Panic

We produce a Figure Chart of Amalgamated Copper showing movements during the 1903 panic and up to the following March (1904). It makes an interesting study. The stock sold early in the year at 75⅝ and the low point reached during the above period was 33⅝. The movements prior to those recorded here show a series of downward steps; but when 36 is reached, the formation changes, and the supporting points are raised. A seven-point rally, a reaction to almost the low figure, and another sixteen-point rally follow.

On this rally the lines 48-49 gradually form the axis and long rows of these figures seem to indicate that plenty of stock is for sale at this level. In case we are not sure as to whether this is further accumulation or distribution we wait until the price shows signs of breaking out of this narrow range. After the second run up to 51 the gradually lowering tops warn us that pressure is resumed. We therefore look for lower prices.

**Interpreting the Chart**

The downward steps continue till 35 is touched, where a 36-7 line begins to form. There is a dip to 33⅝, which gives us the full figure 34, after which the bottoms are higher and lines commence forming at 38-9. Here are all the earmarks of manipulative depression and accumulation—the stock is not allowed to rally over 39 until liquidation is complete. Then the gradually raised bottoms notify us in advance that the stock is about to push through to higher levels.

Now if the Figure Chart were an infallible guide no one would have to learn anything more than its correct interpretation in order to make big money. Our correspondent says, "after a thorough trial of the chart on U. P. I find that I could have made a very considerable sum if I had followed the indications shown." But he would not have followed the indications shown. He is fooling himself. It is easy to look over the chart afterwards and see where he could have made correct plays, but I venture to say he never tested the plan under proper conditions.

Let anyone who thinks he can make money following a Figure Chart or any other kind of a chart have a friend prepare it, keeping secret the name of the stock and the period covered. Then put down on paper a positive set of rules which are to be strictly adhered to, so that there can be no guesswork. Each situation will then call for a certain play and no deviation is to be allowed. Cover up with a sheet of paper all but the beginning of the chart, gradually sliding the paper to the right as you progress. Record each order and execution just as if actually trading. Put Rollo Tape down as coppering every trade and when done send him a check for what you have lost.

**Make a Test**

I have yet to meet the man who has made money trading on a Figure Chart over an extended period.

Any kind of a chart will show some profits at times, but the test is: How much money will it make during several months' operations?

The Figure Chart can be used in other ways. Some people construct figure charts showing each fractional change instead of the full points. The idea may also be used in connection with the Dow, Jones & Co. average prices. But for the practical Tape Reader the full figure chart first described is about the only one we can recommend.

Its value to the Tape Reader lies chiefly in its indications of accumulation and distribution. These frequently (not always) warn the operator in advance of an important move and put him on the watch for the moment when either process is completed and the marking up or down begins.

The chart gives the direction of coming moves; the tape says "when."

Some people claim to be able to predict how far such a movement will go by counting the number of full figures which form an unbroken line. In a case where a stock shows a long horizontal line of 19s and 20s at the bottom of a decline, and a count of the 20s shows that there are twelve of them, this is taken as an indication that there will be a rise of twelve points from 20. Figure charts seem to bear this out in some instances, but like the majority of chart indications, there are very **Many** many exceptions to the rule. There **Exceptions** appears some little foundation for the supposition, however, as it is logical to suppose that the more important the contemplated move, the more stock will the insiders wish to buy and the longer time will be required in which to accumulate it.

The ordinary single line chart which

is so widely used, is valuable chiefly as a compact history of a stock's movements. If the stock which is charted were the only one in the market, its gyrations would be less erratic and its chart, therefore, a more reliable indicator of its trend and destination. But we must keep before us the incontrovertible fact that the movements of every stock are to a greater or lesser extent affected by those of every other stock. This in a large measure accounts for the instability of stock movements as recorded in single line charts.

**Reciprocal Influences**

Then, too, as shown in foregoing studies in this series, one stock may be the lever with which the whole market is being held up, or the club with which the general list is being pounded. A chart of the pivotal stock might give a strong buying indication, whereupon the blind chart devotee would go long to his ultimate regret; for when the concealed distribution was completed his stock would probably break quickly and badly.

This shows clearly the advantage of Tape Reading over chart playing. The Tape Reader sees everything that is going on; the chart player's vision is limited to one issue. Both aim to get in right and go with the trend, but the eye that comprehends the market as a whole is the one which can read this trend most accurately.

## Tape Reading

If one wishes a mechanical trend indicator as a supplement and a guide to his Tape Reading, he had best keep a chart composed of the average daily high and low of eight or ten leading stocks. For convenience in figuring this average it is well to take ten stocks, say Union, Reading, St. Paul, Pennsylvania, N. Y. Central and Erie among the railroads, and Amalgamated, Smelters, Steel and Car Foundry among the industrials. First find the average high and average low for the day and make a chart showing which was touched first. This will be found a more reliable guide than the Dow, Jones averages, which only consider the closing bid of each day, and which, as strongly illustrated in the May, 1901, panic, frequently do not fairly represent the day's actual fluctuations.

**A Composite Chart**

Such a composite chart is of no value to the Tape Reader who scalps and closes out everything daily. But it should benefit those who read the tape for the purpose of catching the important five or ten point moves. Such a trader will make no commitments not in accordance with the trend, as shown by this chart. His reason is that even a well planned bull campaign in a stock will not usually be pushed to completion in the face of a down trend in the general market. Therefore he waits until the trend conforms to his indication.

### The Use of Charts as Guides and Indicators

It seems hardly necessary to say that an up trend in any chart is indicated by consecutive higher tops and bottoms, like stairs going up, and the reverse by repeated steps toward a lower level. A series of tops or bottoms at the same level shows resistance. A protracted zig-zag within a short radius accompanied by very small volume means lifelessness, but with normal or abnormally large volume, accumulation or distribution is more or less evidenced.

There is a style of chart which was originated by "The Analyst," it being especially adapted to the study of volumes. The following rough sketch will give an idea of it:

The Volume Chart

**Volume Chart**

When made to cover a day's movements in a stock, this chart is particularly valuable in showing the quantity of stock absorbed at various levels.

Comparisons are readily made by adding the quantities horizontally. Many other suggestions will be derived from the study of this chart.

**Dividends**

An important point in connection with the making of charts is the treatment of a stock which sells ex-dividend. Many people consider a dividend as equal to a corresponding decline in market price; in fact, the most prominent publisher of charts follows this method. We do not agree. In our opinion when a stock sells ex-dividend the scale should be changed so that the stock will show the same relative position as before the dividend. For instance, if a stock is 138 before a dividend amounting to 2 per cent and sells at 136 ex-dividend, the 138 line becomes the 136 line, etc.

There is another form of chart which is sometimes valuable in detecting the beginning and end of a manipulative campaign. It is based principally on volumes and affords a ready indicator of any unusual activity in a stock. The scale is set at the side to represent the volume and the vertical lines are drawn to show the number of shares for the day. A plus or minus sign at the top of each vertical line may be used to indicate a net advance or decline for the day. Some people add to this an oblique line to show the range for the day.

The proficient Tape Reader will doubtless prefer to discard all mechanical helps, because they interfere with his sensing the trend. Besides, if he keeps the charts himself the very

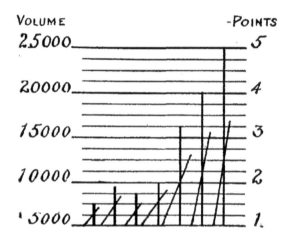

Chart Showing Daily Volume and Width of Swing

act of running them distracts his attention from the tape on which his eye should be constantly riveted. This can of course be overcome by employing an assistant; but taking everything into consideration—the division of attention, the contradictions and the confusing situations which will frequently result—we advise students to stand free of mechanical helps so far as it is possible.

**Stick to the Tape**

Our correspondent in saying "a chart is but a copy of the tape" doubtless refers to the chart of one stock. The full tape cannot possibly be charted. The tape does tell the story, but charting one or two stocks is like recording the actions of one individual as exemplifying the actions of a very large family.

## IX. Daily Trades vs. Long Pull Operations

JUST now I took a small triangular piece of blotting paper three-eighths of an inch at its widest, and stuck it on the end of a pin. I then threw a blot of ink on a paper and put the blotter into contact. The ink fairly jumped up into the blotter, leaving the paper comparatively dry.

This is exactly how the market acts on the tape when its absorptive powers are greater than the supply—large quantities are taken at the offered prices and at the higher levels. Prices leap forward. The demand seems insatiable.

After two or three blots had thus been absorbed, the botter would take no more. It was thoroughly saturated. Its demands were satisfied. Just in this way the market comes to a standstill at the top of a rise and hangs there. Supply and demand are equalized at the new price level.

Then I filled my pen with ink, and let the fluid run off the point and onto the blotter. (This illustrated the distribution of stocks in the market.) Beyond a certain point the blotter would take no more. A drop formed and fell to the paper. (Supply exceeded demand.) The more I put on the blotter the faster fell the drops. (Liquidation—market seeking a lower level.)

This is a simple way of fixing in our minds the principal opposing forces that are constantly operating in the market—absorption and distribution, demand and supply, support and pressure. The more adept a Tape Reader becomes in weighing and measuring these elements, the more successful he will be.

But he must remember that even his most accurate readings will often be nullified by events which are transpiring every moment of the day. His stock may start upward with a rush—apparently there is power enough to carry it several points; but after advancing a couple of points it may run up against a larger quantity of stock than can be obsorbed, or some unforeseen incident may change the whole complexion of the market. The Tape Reader must be quick to detect such changes, switch his position and go with this newly formed trend.

**Watchfulness**

To show how an operator may be caught twice on the wrong side in one day and still come out ahead, let us look at the tape of December 21, 1908.

Union Pacific opened below the previous night's close: 500 . 179 . 6000 .

178¾ and for the first few moments looked as though there was some inside support. Supposing the Tape Reader had

BOUGHT 100 UNION PACIFIC AT 178⅞, he would have soon noticed fresh selling orders in sufficient volume to produce weakness. Upon this he would have immediately

SOLD 200 UNION PACIFIC AT 178¼, putting him short one hundred at the latter price. The weakness increased and after a drive to 176½, two or three warnings were given that the pressure was temporarily off. A comparatively strong undertone developed in Southern Pacific as well as other stocks and short covering began in Union Pacific, which came 600 . 176⅝ . 1000 . ¾, then 177¼. Assuming that the operator considered this the turn, he would have

A Mistake

BOUGHT 200 UNION PACIFIC AT 176⅞, which was the next quotation. This would have put him long. Thereafter the market showed more resiliency, but only small lots appeared on the tape.

A little later the market quiets down. The rally does not hold well. He expects the stock to react again to the low point. This it does, but it fails to halt there; it goes driving through to 176, accompanied by considerable weakness in the other active stocks. This is his indication that fresh liquidation has started.   So he

SELLS 200 UNION PACIFIC AT 176.
That is   he dumps over his long and goes short at 176.

The weakness continues and there is no sign of a rally until after the stock has struck 174½.   This being a break of 6¼ points since yesterday, the Tape Reader is now wide awake for signs of a turn, realizing that every additional fraction brings him nearer to that point, wherever it may be.

After touching 174½ the trend of the market changes completely.  Larger lots are in demand at the offered prices.  There is a final drive but very little stock comes out on it.  During this drive he

**Catching the Turn**

BUYS 100 UNION PACIFIC AT 174⅞,

and as signs of a rally multiply he

BUYS 100 UNION PACIFIC AT 175¼.

From that moment it is easy sailing. There is ample opportunity for him to unload his last purchase just before the close when he

SELLS 100 UNION PACIFIC AT 176⅝.

| Bought. | Sold. | Loss. | Profit. |
|---------|-------|-------|---------|
| 178⅞ | 178¼ | $62.50 | ...... |
| 176⅞ | 178¼ | ...... | $137.50 |
| 176⅞ | 176 | 87.50 | ...... |
| 174⅞ | 176 | ...... | 112.50 |
| 175¼ | 176⅝ | ...... | 137.50 |
| Commissions and taxes...... | | 135.00 | ...... |
| | | $285.00 | $387.50 |
| | | | 285.00 |

Net profit for the day .................. $102.50

This is doing very well considering he was caught twice on the wrong side and in his wigglings paid $135 in commissions and taxes.

Success in trading being chiefly a question of reducing and eliminating losses, commissions, interest and revenue stamps, let us see whether he might have used better judgment. His first trade seems to have been made on what appeared to be inside buying. No trend had developed. He saw round lots being taken at 178¼ and over and reasoned that a rally should naturally follow pronounced support. His mistake was in not waiting for a clearly defined trend. If the buying was strong enough to absorb all offerings and turn the market, he would have done better to have waited till this was certain. When a stock holds steady within a half point radius it does not signify a reversal of trend, but rather a halting place from which a new move in either direction may begin.

**Waiting for the Trend**

Had he followed the first sharp move, his original trade would have been on the short—not the long side. This would have saved him his first loss with its attendant expenses, aggregating $89.50, and would have nearly doubled the day's profits.

His second loss was made on a trade which involved one of the finest points in the art of Tape Reading, viz., that of distinguishing a rally from a change in trend. A good way to do this successfully is to figure where a stock is due to come after it makes an upturn, allowing that a normal rally is from one-half to two-thirds of the decline. That is, when a stock declines two and a half points we can look for at least a point and a quarter rally unless the pressure is still on. In case the decline is not over, the rally will fall short.

**Distinguishing a Mere Rally**

What did Union do after it touched 176½? It sold at 176⅝ . ¾ . 177¼. Having declined from 179⅛ to 176½, 2⅝ points, it was due to rally at least 1¼ points, or to 177¾. Its failing to make this figure indicated that the decline was not over and that his short position should be maintained.

Furthermore, that last jump of half a point between sales showed an un-healthy condition of the market. For a few moments there was evidently a cessation of selling, then somebody reached for a hundred shares offered at 177¼. As the next sale was 176⅞ the hollowness of the rise became apparent.

While this rally lasted, the lots were small. This of itself was reason for not covering. Had a genuine demand sprung from either longs or shorts a steady rise, on increasing volumes, would have taken place. The absence of such indications seems to us now a reason for not covering and going long at 176⅞.

## Daily Trades vs. Long Pull Operations

It is very difficult for anyone to say what he would actually have done under the circumstances, but had both these trades been avoided for the reasons mentioned, the profit for the day would have been $421, as the 100 sold at 178¼ would have been covered at 174⅞, and the long at 175¼ sold out at 176⅝. So we can see the advantage of studying our losses and mistakes, with a view to benefiting in future transactions.

**Studying Losses**

As previously explained, the number of dollars profit is subordinate to whether the trader can make profits at all and whether the points made exceed the points lost. With success from this standpoint it is only a question of increased capital enabling one to enlarge his trading unit.

A good way to watch the progress of an account is to keep a book showing dates, quantities, prices, profits and losses, also commission, tax and interest charges. Beside each trade should be entered the number of points net profit or loss, together with a running total showing just how many points the account is ahead or behind. A chart of these latter figures will prevent anyone fooling himself as to his progress. People are too apt to remember their profits and forget their losses.

The losses taken by an expert Tape Reader are so small that he can trade in much larger units than one who is

**Small Losses**

away from the tape or who is trading with an arbitrary stop. The Tape Reader will seldom take over half a point to a point loss for the reason that he will generally buy or sell at, or close to, the pivotal point or the line of resistance. Therefore, should the trend of his stock suddenly reverse, he is with it in a moment. The losses in the above mentioned Union Pacific transactions (⅝ and ⅞ respectively) are perhaps a fair average, but frequently he will be able to trade with a risk of only ¼, ⅜ or ½.

The fact that this possible loss is confined to a fraction should not lead him to trade too frequently. It is better to look on part of the time; to rest the mind and allow the judgment to clarify. Dull days will often constrain one for a time and are therefore beneficial.

The big money in Tape Reading is made during very active markets. Big swings and large volumes produce unmistakable indications and a harvest for the experienced operator. He welcomes twenty, thirty and fifty-point moves in stocks like Reading, Union or Consolidated Gas—powerful plays by financial giants.

And this fact reminds us of one of the things we have heretofore intended to reason out: Is it better to close trades each day, or hold through reactions, and if necessary, for several days or weeks in order to secure a large profit?

The answer to this question depends somewhat upon the temperament of the Tape Reader. If his make-up is such that he can closely follow the small swings with profit, gradually becoming more expert and steadily increasing his commitments, he will shortly "arrive" by that route. If his disposition is such that he cannot trade in and out actively, but is content to wait for big opportunities and patient enough to hold on for large profits, he will also "get there." It is impossible to say which style of trading would produce the best average results, because it depends altogether upon individual qualifications.

Looking at the question broadly, we should say that the Tape Reader who understood the lines thus far suggested in this series, might find it both difficult and less profitable to operate solely for the long swings. In the first place, he would be obliged to let twenty or thirty opportunities pass by to every one that he would accept. The small swings of one to three points greatly outnumber the five and ten-point movements, and there would be a considerable percentage of losing trades no matter how he operated.

It would seem also that close contact with the ticker would not give the correct perspective for long pull

*Difference in Individuals*

operations. Many of the indications, such as the extent of reactions, lines of resistance, etc., will be found equally operative in the broader swings, just as an enlargement of a photograph retains the lines of its original. Tape Reading seems essentially a profession for the man who is mentally active and flexible, capable of making quick and accurate decisions and keenly sensitive to the most minute indications. On the other hand, trading for the larger swings requires one to ignore the minor prognostics, and to put some stress upon the influential news of the day, and its effect upon sentiment; he must stand ready to take larger losses and in many ways handle himself in a manner altogether different from that of the small swing trader.

**Trading for the Long Swings**

The more closely we look at the proposition, the more the two methods of operating seem to disunite, the broad swing plan appearing best adapted to those who are not in continuous touch with the ticker and who therefore have the advantage of distance and perspective.

*In a subsequent series we hope to take up this subject in detail, in an effort to show how the business and the professional man who cannot attend his broker's office, may profitably apply intelligent foresight to the stock market under the shade of his evening lamp.*

## Daily Trades vs. Long Pull Operations

There is no reason why the Tape Reader should not make long swing trading an auxiliary profit producer if he can keep such trades from influencing his daily operations.

Auxiliary Trades

For example, in the recent shake-down on Reading from 144⅜ to 118, on his first buying indication he could have taken on an extra lot for the long swing, knowing that if the turn had really been made, a rally to over 130 was due. A stop order would have limited his risk and conserved his profits as they rolled up and there is no telling how much of the subsequent forty point rise he might have secured.

Another case was when Steel broke from 58¾ last November (1908) to 41¼ in February. The market at the time was hinging on Steel and it was likely that the Tape Reader would be operating in it. His first long trade under this plan would be for at least a hundred shares more than his usual amount, with a stop on the long pull lot at say 40¾. He would naturally expect a rally of at least 8¾ points (to 50), but would, in a sense, forget this hundred shares, so long as the market showed no signs of another important decline. When it reached 60 he might still be holding it.

The above are merely a couple of opportunities from recent stock market history. Dozens of such openings show themselves every year and should form no small part of the Tape Reader's income. But he must separate such trades from his regular daily trading; to allow them to conflict would destroy the effectiveness of both. If he finds the long pull trade interfering with the accuracy of his judgment, he should close it out at once. He must play on one side of the fence if he cannot operate on both.

**A Dual Capacity**

One can readily foresee how a trader with one hundred shares of Steel at 43 for the long pull, and two hundred for the day, would be tempted to close out all three hundred on indications of a decline. This is where he can test his ability to act in a dual capacity. He must ask himself: Have I good reason for thinking Steel will sell down five points before up five? Is this a small reaction or a big shakedown? Are we still in a bull swing? Has the stock had its normal rally from the last decline? These and many other questions will enable him to decide whether he should hold this hundred shares or clean house.

It takes an exceptionaly strong will and clear head to act in this way without interfering with one's regular trading. Anyone can sell two hundred and hold one hundred; but will his judgment be biased because he is simultaneously long and short—bullish and bearish? There's the rub!

The real Tape Reader is apt to prefer a clean slate at 3 P. M. every day, so that he can sit down to his ticker at the next morning's opening and say, "I have no commitments and no opinion. I will follow the first strong indication." He would rather average $100 a day for ten days than make $1,000 on one trade in the same length of time. The risk is generally limited to a fraction and having arrived at a point where he is showing even small average daily profits, his required capital per 100 shares need not be over $1,500 to $2,000.

Suppose for sixty days on 100-share operations his average profits over losses were only a quarter of a point—$25 a day. At the end of that time his capital would have been increased by $1,500, enabling him to trade in 200 share lots. Another thirty days with similar results and he could trade in 300-share lots, and so on. I do not mention these figures for any other purpose than to again emphasize that the objective point in Tape Reading is not large individual profits, but a continuous chipping in of small average net profits per day.

About two months ago, I am told, a man from the West came into the office of THE TICKER, and said that he had been impressed by this series on Tape Reading, and had come to New York for the sole purpose of trying his hand at it. He had $1,000 which

he was willing to lose in demonstra
ting whether he was fitted for the
work.

He was advised not to trade in over
ten-share lots, and was especially
warned against operating at all until
after he had actually studied the tape
for two or three months.

Recently, I am informed, he called
again and related some of his experi-
ences. It seems that he could not ab-
stain from trading, but started within two or three days after he decided
on a brokerage house. He stated that
during the two months he had made
forty-two trades of ten shares each and
had never had on hand over twenty
full shares at any one time. He admitted that he had frequently mixed
guesswork and tips with his Tape
Reading, but as a rule he had followed
the tape.

His losses were seldom over a point
and his greatest loss was one and a
half points. His maximum profit was
three points. He had at times traded
in other stocks beside the leaders. In
spite of his inexperience, and his attempt to mix tips and guesses with
shrewd judgment, he was actually
ahead of the game, after paying out
about $125 in commissions, etc.

This was especially surprising in
view of the trader's market through
which he had passed. While the
amount of his net profit was small,

the fact that he had shown any profit under the circumstances was reason enough for congratulation.

Another handicap which he did not perhaps realize was his environment. He had been trading in an office where he could hear and see what everyone else was doing, and where news, gossip and opinions were freely and openly expressed by many people. All these things tended to influence him, and to switch him from his Tape Reading.

I have no doubt that having mastered the art of cutting losses and keeping commitments down, he will soon overcome his other deficiencies. Given a broad, active market, he should show increasing average daily profits.

**Cutting Losses**

He is creeping now. By-and-by he will know how to walk.

Speculation is a business. It must be learned.

## X. Various Examples and Suggestions

RECENT trading observations and experiments have convinced me that it is impracticable and almost impossible to gauge the extent of a movement by its initial fluctuations.

Gauging the Swing

Many important swings begin in the most modest way. The top of an important decline may present nothing more than a light volume and a drifting tendency toward lower prices, subsequently developing into a heavy, slumpy market, and ending in a violent downward plunge.

In a previous number I suggested that the Tape Reader select only those moves which seem to offer opportunities for wide swings. My opinion now is that the operator should aim to catch every important swing in the leading active stock. To do this he must act promptly when a stock goes into a new field or otherwise gives an indication, and he must be ready to follow wherever it leads. If it has been moving within a three-point radius and suddenly takes on new life and activity, bursting through its former bounds, he must go with it.

I do not mean that he should try to catch every wriggle. If the stock rises three points and then reverses one or one and a half points on light volume, he must look upon it as a perfectly natural reaction and not a change of trend. The expert operator will not ordinarily let all of three points get away from him. He will keep pushing his stop up behind until the first good reaction puts him out at close to the high figure. This leaves him in a position to repurchase on the reaction, provided no better opportunity presents itself. Having purchased at such a time, he will sell out again as the price once more approaches the high figure, unless indications point to its forging through to a new high level.

Every movement of the market and of each stock passes through stages corresponding to those in the life of an individual, aptly described by my old college chum, Bill Shakespeare, as "The Seven Ages." The Tape Reader aims to get in during Infancy and out at Old Age.

**Stages of Market Movements**

Usually a movement gives signs when it begins to totter. A recent example was given in the rise in Union Pacific about June 21st to 23d (1909), when the stock rose from 187⅞ to 194⅝, accompanied by an abnormal advance in the preferred. Each morning the London price for both issues came higher and there was persistent buying all day in the New York market. After touching 194⅝ the movement completely fizzled out. Buying pressure ceased. The preferred reacted sharply, and the common came back to 193⅞. Thereafter its rallies were feeble, the pressure was all on the down side, and today, June 26th, it is still heavy at 191⅞.

A new bull movement may have its birth during great weakness or pressure. Just prior to the above time, Reading was pounded down to 147⅝, then to 147¼, and the resistance which it offered at this level gave notice that a new swing was about to be inaugurated. These were signs that the Tape Reader had better get bullish. Purchases could have been made with only a fractional risk, and subsequent profits were chiefly on the bull side. Two or three days later the price touched 155½, then it went above 158.

**Importance of Volumes**

The more we study volumes, the better we appreciate their value in Tape Reading. It frequently occurs that a stock will work within a three-point range for days at a time without giving one a chance for a respectable-sized scalp. Without going out of these boundaries, it suddenly begins coming out on the tape in thousands instead of hundreds. This is evidence that a new movement has started, but not necessarily in the direction which is first indicated. The Tape Reader must immediately go with the trend, but until it is clearly defined and the stock breaks through its former limits with large and increasing volumes, he must exercise great caution. The reason is this: If the stock has been suddenly advanced, it may be for the purpose of facilitating sales by a large operator. The Tape is the most suggestive thing in the world. A sharp rise of this kind induces a number of people to buy; their buying attracts others and as the tide swells it carries all before it until everybody throws caution aside and jumps in. Thus we see a cross section of a pyramid formed by outsiders working *en masse*. A legitimate movement of this kind will frequently run several points. The large operator who wishes to unload a block of stock or put out a big line of shorts, creates an illegitimate move, inducing others to buy and making a market for what he wishes to dispose of. The best way to distinguish the genuine from the fictitious move is to watch out for abnormally large volumes within a small radius. This usually evidences washed sales and other manipulations. The large volume is simply a means of attracting buyers and disguising the hand of the operator.

Cross
Section of
a Movement

A play of this kind took place the

last time Reading struck 159¾ (June, 1909). I counted some 80,000 shares within about half a point of 159—unmistakable notice of a coming decline. This was a case where the stock was put up before being put down, and the Tape Reader who interpreted the move correctly and played for a good down swing would have made considerable money.

We frequently hear people complaining that "the public is not in this market," as though that were a reason why stocks should not go up or the market should be avoided. The speaker is usually one of those who constitute "the public," but he regards the expression as signifying "every outsider except myself." In the judgment of many the market is better off without the public. To be sure, brokers do not enjoy so large a business, the fluctuations are not so riotous, but the market moves in an orderly way and responds more accurately to prevailing conditions.

**The Public**

A market in which the public predominates represents a sort of speculative "jag" indulged in by those whose stock market knowledge should be rated at ⅛. Everyone recognizes the fact that when the smoke clears away, the Street is full of victims who didn't know how and couldn't wait to learn. Their plungings produce violent fluctuations, however, and in this respect are of advantage to the Tape Reader who would much rather see ten-point than three-point swings.

To offset this, there are some disadvantages. First, in a market where there is "rioting of accumulated margins," the tape is so far behind that it is seldom one can secure an execution at anywhere near his price. This is especially true when activity breaks out in a stock which has been comparatively dull. So many people with money, watching the tape, are attracted by these apparent opportunities, that the scramble to get in results in every one paying more than he figured; thus the Tape Reader finds it impossible to know where he is at until he gets his report. His tape prices are five minutes stale and his broker is so busy it takes four or five minutes for an execution instead of one or two minutes.

**Execution of Orders**

In the next place, stop orders are often filled at from small fractions to points away from his stop price—there is no telling what figure he will get, while in ordinary markets he can place his stops within $\frac{1}{4}$ of a resistance point and frequently have the price come within $\frac{1}{8}$ of his stop without catching it.

So it is a question whether, all things considered, the presence of the public is a help or a detriment to successful Tape Reading.

**Stop Orders**

Speaking of stop orders: The ways in which one may manipulate his stops for protection and advantage, become more numerous as experience is acquired. Remembering that the Tape Reader is operating for a fractional average profit per trade, or per day, he cannot afford to let a point profit run into a loss, or fail to "plug" a larger profit at a point where at least a portion of it will be preserved.

One of my recent day's trading will illustrate this idea. I had just closed out a couple of trades, in which there had been losses totaling slightly over a point. Both were on the long side. The market began to show signs of a break, and singling out Reading as the most vulnerable, I got short of it at 150¾. In a few moments it sold below 150. My stop was moved down so there couldn't be a loss, and soon a slight rally and another break gave me a new stop which insured a profit, come what might. A third drive started, and I pushed the stop down to within ¼ of the tape price at the time, as it was late in the day and I considered this the final plunge. By the time my order reached the floor the price was well away from this latest stop and when the selling became most violent I told my broker to cover "at the market." The price paid was within ¼ of the bottom for the day, and netted 2⅝ after commissions were paid.

## Various Examples and Suggestions

I strongly advocate this method of profit insuring. The scientific elimination of loss is one of the most important factors in the art, and the operator who fails to properly protect his paper profits will find that many a point which he thought he had cinched has slipped away from him.

It is also a question whether, in such a case, the trade had better not be stopped out than closed out. When you push a stop close behind a rise or a decline, you leave the way open for a further profit; but when you close the trade of your own volition, you shut off all such chances. If it is your habit to close out everything before three o'clock daily, the stop may be placed closer than ordinarily during the last fifteen minutes of the session, and when a sharp move in the desired direction occurs, the closing out may be done by a stop only a fraction away from the extreme price. This whole plan of using stops is a sort of squeezing out the last drop of profit from each trade and never losing any part that can possibly be retained.

Suppose the operator sells a stock short at 53 and it breaks to 51. He is foolish not to bring his stop down to 51¼ unless the market is ripe for a heavy decline. With his stop at this point he has two chances out of three that the result will be satisfactory: (1) The price may go lower and yield a further profit; (2) The normal rally to 52 will catch his stop and enable him to put the stock out again at that price. The third contingency is that it will rally to about 51¼, catch his stop and then go lower. He can scarcely mourn over the loss of a further profit in such a case.

**Scalping on Both Sides**

If the stock refuses to rally the full point to which it is entitled, that is, if it comes up to 51½ or ⅝ and still acts heavy, it may be expected to break lower, and there usually is ample time to get short again at a price that will at least cover commissions.

There is nothing more confusing than to attempt scalping on both sides of the market at once. You may go long of a stock which is being put up or is going up for some special reason, and short of another stock which is persistently weak. Both trades may pan out successfully, but meantime the judgment will be interfered with and some foolish mistake will be made in four cases out of five. As Dickson G. Watts said, "Act so as to keep the mind clear, the judgment trustworthy." The mind is not clear when the trader is working actively on two opposing sides of the market. A bearish indication is favorable to one trade, and unfavorable to the other. He finds himself interpreting every development as being to his advantage and forgetting the important fact that he is also on the opposite side.

It is much better if you are short of one stock and see another that looks like a purchase, to wait until you have covered your short trade (on a dip if possible), and then take the long side of the other issue. The best time for both covering and going long is on a recession which in such a case serves a double purpose. The mind should be made up in advance as to which deal offers the best chance for profit, so that when the moment for action arrives there will be nothing to do but act.

This is one great advantage the Tape Reader has over other operators who do not employ market science. By a process of elimination he decides which side of the market and which stock affords the best opportunity. He **Getting in** either gets in at the inception of a movement or waits for the first reaction after the move has started. He knows just about where his stock will come on the reaction and judges by the way it then acts whether his first impression is confirmed or nullified. After he gets in it must come up to expectations or he should abandon the trade. If it is a bull move, the volume must increase and the rest of the market offer some support or at least not oppose it. The reactions must show a smaller volume than the advances, indicating light pressure, and each upward swing must be of longer duration and reach a new high level, or it will mean that the rise has spent its force either temporarily or finally.

Tape Reading is the only known method of trading which gets you in at the beginning, keeps you posted throughout the move, and gets you out when it has culminated.

**Advantages of Tape Reading**

If anything more approaching perfection in this regard exists will someone kindly come to the front with it?

Has anyone ever heard of a man, a method, system, or anything else that that will do this for you in Wall Street?

It has made fortunes for the comparatively few who have followed it.

It is an art in which one can become highly expert and more and more successful as practice and experience sandpapers his work and shows him what to avoid.

I should like to hear from my readers who have followed this series, whether they have been operating under its guidance or not. I should like to know how many have started to perfect themselves in Tape Reading, and how many have been aided indirectly; what portions and which ideas have benefited them most; what points are not clear or still uncovered. Please write me fully and I will try to answer in the two subsequent numbers, which will close the series. Address Rollo Tape, care of THE TICKER.

## XI.  Obstacles to be Overcome— Possible Profits

**M**ENTAL poise is an indispensable factor in Tape Reading. The mind should be absolutely free to concentrate upon the work; there should be no feeling that certain things are to be accomplished within a given time; no fear, anxiety or ambition.

When a Tape Reader has his emotions well in hand, he will play as though the game were dominoes. When anything interferes with this attitude it should be eliminated. If, for example, there be an unusual series of losses, the trader had better suspend operations until he discovers the cause.

Following are some of the obstacles which are likely to be encountered:

**Trading Too Often**

1. One may be trading too often. Many opportunities for profit develop from each day's movements; only the very choicest should be acted upon. There should be no haste. The market will be there to-morrow in case to-day's opportunities do not meet requirements.

2. Anxiety to make a record, to avoid losses, to secure a certain profit for the

day or period will greatly warp the judgment, and lead to a low percentage of profits. Tape Reading is a good deal like laying eggs. If the hen is not left to pick up the necessary foods and retire in peace to her nest, she will not produce properly. If she is worried by dogs and small boys, or tries to lay seven eggs out of material for six, the net proceeds may look like an omelet.

The Tape Reader's profits should develop naturally. He should buy or sell because it is the thing to do—not because he wants to make a profit or fears to make a loss.

3. The market may be unsuited to Tape Reading operations. When prices drift up and down without trend, like a ship without a rudder, and few positive indications develop, the percentage of losing trades is apt to be high. When this condition continues it is well to hold off until the character of the market changes.

4. One's broker may be giving poor service. In a game as fine as this, every fraction counts. Executions of market orders should average not over two minutes. Stop orders should be reported in less time as such orders are on the floor and at the proper post when they become operative. By close attention to details in the handling of my orders, I have been able to reduce the average time of my executions to less than one minute. The quickest report obtained

**Poor Service**

thus far required but twenty-five seconds. To the best of my knowledge this is a record for New York Stock Exchange executions of orders given from an office.

A considerable portion of my orders are executed in from thirty to forty seconds, varying according to whether my broker is near the 'phone or in a distant crowd when the orders reach the floor and how far the definitive "crowd" is from his 'phone.

I have arranged a special order slip which distinguishes my orders. It reads:

Special
Order Slip

> # BUY AT THE OFFERED PRICE AND
> # REPORT INSTANTLY

## Obstacles to Be Overcome

The selling slips read, *"Sell at the bid price and report instantly."* Such orders leave nothing to the discretion of the broker. He cannot "try to do better" than the momentary bid or offered price. Like Paddy at the wake, his business is to "hit the first man who opens his mouth."

Ordinarily it is expected and is really an advantage to the general run of speculators to have the broker use some discretion; that is, try to do better, providing there is no chance of losing his market. But I do not wish my broker to act thus for me. My indications usually show me the exact moment when a stock should be bought or sold and a few moments' delay often means a good many dollars lost.

**The Broker's Discretion**

With the execution of orders reduced to a matter of seconds, I can also hold stop orders in my own hands and when the stop price is reached, 'phone the order to buy or sell at the market. Results are very satisfactory as my own broker handles the orders and not the specialist or some other floor broker.

To return to the question of mental equilibrium, the Tape Reader should be careful to trade only in such amounts as will not interfere with his judgment. If he finds that a series of losses upsets him it is an easy matter to reduce the number of shares one-half or a quarter of the regular amount, or even to ten shares so that the dollars involved are no longer a factor. This gives him a chance for a little self-examination.

If a person is in poor physical condition or his mental alertness below par for any reason, he may be unable to stand the excitement attending the work. Loss of sleep, for example, may render one unfit to carry all the quotations in his head, or to plan and execute his moves quickly and accurately. When anything of this kind occurs which prevents the free play of all the faculties it is best to bring the day's work to a close.

**Fractional Profits**

Some of my readers think it futile to aim for a fractional average profit per trade when there are many full points per day to be made by holding on through days and weeks and getting full benefit of the big moves. Admitting that it is possible to make many more points at times there is a risk of losses corresponding to the profits and the question is not how much we can *make,* but how much we can make *net.*

Tape Reading reduces profit-making to a manufacturing basis.

To show how the nimble eighths pile up when their cumulative power is fully employed, I have prepared a table representing the results of 250 trading days, starting with a capital of $1,000. It is assumed that the Tape Reader has reached that stage of expertness where he can average one trade a day and a profit of $12.50 per trade, and that as fast as

$1,000 is accumulated he adds 100 shares to his trading unit.

I can hear the expressions of those who look over these figures: "Oh! That looks all very well on paper, but wait till it comes to doing it in the market."

These results depend solely upon the Tape Reader's ability to make ⅛ more than he loses per day. There is no limit to the number of shares he can trade in, provided he has the margin. If he is at all proficient his margin will not be depleted more than a few points before he makes up his losses and more. He is not pyramiding in the ordinary sense of the word; he is simply doing an increasing volume of shares as his capital expands. All progressive business men increase commitments as fast as warranted by their capital and opportunities.

The Nimble Eighth

What a profit of 1-8 per day would amount to in 250 days if profits were used as additional margin.

| 100 shares | $12.50 a day | $1,000.00 in | 80 days |
|---|---|---|---|
| 200 " | 25.00 " | 1,000.00 " | 40 " |
| 300 " | 37.50 " | 1,012.50 " | 27 " |
| 400 " | 50.00 " | 1,000.00 " | 20 " |
| 500 " | 62.50 " | 1,000.00 " | 16 " |
| 600 " | 75.00 " | 1,050.00 " | 14 " |
| 700 " | 87.50 " | 1,050.00 " | 12 " |
| 800 " | 100.00 " | 1,000.00 " | 10 " |
| 900 " | 112.50 " | 1,012.50 " | 9 " |
| 1000 " | 125.00 " | 1,000.00 " | 8 " |
| 1100 " | 137.50 " | 962.50 " | 7 " |
| 1200 " | 150.00 " | 1,050.00 " | 7 " |

$12,137.50 "    250 "

Less tax ................1,942.00

Net profit .................$10,195.50

Assuming that there are about three hundred Stock Exchange sessions in the year, the two hundred and fifty days figured represent five-sixths of a year or ten months. From 'that time on, having struck his gait, the Tape Reader can, without increasing his unit to over 1200 shares, make $900 a week or $46,800 a year.

**Overcoming the "Kitty"**

One trader who for years has been trying to scalp the market and who could never quite overcome the "kitty," reports that his first attempts at applying these rules resulted in a loss of about $20 per trade. This he gradually reduced to $12, then to $8, finally succeeding in throwing the balance over to the credit side and is now able to make a daily profit of from $12 to $30 per 100 shares. This is doing very well indeed. I have no doubt that his profits will continue to increase.

Some people seem to hold the opinion that as the profits desired are only $\frac{1}{8}$ average per trade one should limit himself in taking profits. Perhaps I have not made myself clear in this respect.

I buy and sell when I get my indications. In going into a trade I do not know whether it will show a profit or a loss, or how much. I try to trade at a point where I can secure protection with a stop from $\frac{1}{4}$ to $\frac{1}{2}$ point away, so that my risk is limited to this fraction plus commission and tax. If the trade goes in my favor I push the stop up as soon as possible, to a point where there can be no loss.

I do not let profits run blindly but only so long as there appears no indication on which to close. No matter where my stop order stands, I am always on the watch for danger signals. Sometimes I get them way in advance of the time a trade should be closed; in other instances my "get out" will flash onto the tape as suddenly and as clearly defined as a streak of lightning against a black sky.

When the tape says "get out" I never stop to reckon how much profit or loss I have or whether I am ahead or behind on the day. I strive for an increasing average profit but I do not keep my eye so much on the fractions or points made or lost, so much as on myself.

I endeavor to perfect myself in clearheadedness, quickness of thought, accuracy of judgment, promptness in planning and executing my plays, foresight, intuition, courage and initiative. Masterful control of myself in these respects will produce a winning average—it is merely a question of practice.

To show how accurately the method works out in practice, I will describe one recent day's trading in which there were three transactions, involving six orders (three buying and three selling). *The market did not go one-eighth against me in five orders out of the six.* In the

Taking Profits

sixth, the stock went ⅝ above the selling price at which my order was given. I have never seen nor heard of this feat being accomplished before by anyone in Wall Street. Details follow:

I had no open trades. Kansas City Southern, which had been intensely dull, came on the tape 2600 at 46¾. I gave a buying order and before it could reach the "post" the Tape said 46⅞ and 47. The stock rose steadily and after selling at 48⅝ and coming back to 48½ I gave the selling order. It has not touched 48⅝ again up to now.

Successful Trades

The next trade was in Reading. I saw that it was being held in check in spite of its great strength. The stock had opened at 158. After a certain bulge I saw the reaction coming. When it arrived, and the stock was selling at 157½, I gave the buying order, got mine at 157⅝ and it has not been there since. It immediately rose to 158¾. I noted selling indications and gave the order while the stock was at that price on the tape. It did not react sufficiently to warrant my picking it up again and later went to 159⅜, which was ⅝ above my selling indication.

Southern Pacific suddenly loomed up as a winner and I bought it at 135. It promptly went to 135½. The rest of the market began to look temporarily over-bulled, so I gave my order to sell when the stock was 135½, which proved to be the highest for the day, making the fifth time out of six orders when my stock moved almost instantly in my favor.

This illustration is not prompted by egotism. It is given as an example of the high percentage of accuracy possible under this method of trading. I do not pretend to be able to accomplish these results except occasionally, but I am constantly striving toward being able to do so in a large percentage of my trades.

If one makes $2\frac{3}{8}$ points one day and loses 2 points in the next two days, he is $\frac{3}{8}$ ahead for the three days, or an average of $\frac{1}{8}$ per day. He may have losing and winning streaks, get discouraged and lose his nerve at times, but if he is made of the right stuff he will in time overcome all obstacles and land at the desired goal.

## XII. Closing the Trades—Suggestions for Students

THE student of Tape Reading, especially he who puts his knowledge into actual practice, is constantly evolving new ideas and making discoveries which modify or nullify his former methods. From each new elevation he enjoys a broader view; what were obstacles disappear; his problems gradually simplify.

We have previously defined Tape Reading as the art of determining the *immediate* trend of prices. If one can do this successfully in the majority of his trades, his profits should roll up. But scenting the trend and getting in right is only one-half of the business. Knowing when to close a trade is just as important, if not the most important part of a complete transaction.

**Losses in Closing**

At a certain point in my trading, I became aware that a large percentage of my losing trades resulted from failure to close at the culmination of what I have termed the immediate trend. An example will make this clear: New

York Central was on a certain day the strongest stock in a bull market which showed a tendency to react. The pressure was on Reading and Steel. My indications were all bullish, so I couldn't consistently sell either of the latter short. I was looking for an opportunity to buy. The market began to slide off, Reading and Steel being the principal clubs with which the pounding was done. I watched them closely and the moment I saw that the selling of these two stocks had ceased, gave my order to buy New York Central, getting it at 137¼. It never touched there again, and in ten minutes was 139 bid for 5,000 shares. Here I should have sold, as my buying indication was for that particular advance. Especially should I have sold when I saw the rise culminate in a spectacular bid which looked like bait for outside buyers. Of course the stock might have gone higher. The main trend for the day was upward. But for the time being 139 was the high point. I knew the stock was due to react from this figure, and it did, but at the bottom of the normal reaction selling broke out in fresh quarters and the whole market came down heavily. The result was that my profit was only a fraction of what it ought to have been.

This is the way the trade might have been made: I should have sold when 139 was noisily bid, and when

**An Error**

the reaction had run its course, picked it up again, provided indications were still bullish. If they were not I would have been in the position of looking to get short instead of waiting for a chance to get out of my long.

Having reserved in the early part of this series the right to revise my views, I will here record the claim that the best results in Tape Reading lie in scenting the moves which are likely to occur in, say, the next half hour, getting in when they start and out when they culminate. This will in most cases cause failure to get *all* of the moves in the one most active stock for the day, but should result in many small profits, and I believe the final results will exceed those realized by sitting on one stock through reactions.

Objections to the latter method are many. One is, the change in leadership which frequently occurs several times during the same session. It being the purpose of the Tape Reader to keep in the leading stock, he must aim to shift from one issue to another as they come to the front.

It is exasperating to see your stock lose its prominence and "turn dead" on your hands, especially if it occurs at a point where part of the profit has disappeared. And there is little comfort in a half-point profit when some other issue would have shown three

**Taking Quick Profits**

**Changes in Leadership**

times as much. Each day's session should be made to yield the highest possible amount of revenue, just as though it were the last day on which trading could be done, and there seems no better way of obtaining these results than by the latest and most approved method mentioned above.

The decks are thus kept clear for whatever offers; there is no dead wood about.

Keeping the
Decks Clear

There is a very wide difference in mental attitude between the man who feels compelled to get out of something and one who is long of money and looking for a chance to make a fresh trade.

The start and finish of one of these small swings is best illustrated by a triangle, the narrow end representing the commencement, and the wide end the culmination. An upward move would appear thus:

and a downward move thus:

These figures denote the widening character of a move as it progresses and are intended to show how volume, activity and number of transactions expand until, at the end, comparatively riotous conditions prevail. The principle works the same in the larger swings; witness the spectacular rise in Union Pacific within a few sessions marking the end of the August, 1909, boom.

**Getting Ready**

After closing out a trade the tape will tell on the following reaction whether you are justified in taking the same stock on again or whether some other issue will pay better. Frequently a stock will be seen preparing for a move two or three swings ahead of the one in which it becomes the leader. This is a fine point, but with study and practice the most complicated indications clarify.

And now a word about the many who are endeavoring to turn this series to practical account. The results which are attainable depend solely upon the individual. Each must work out his own method of trading, based on suggestions derived from these Studies or from other sources. It will doubtless be found that what is one man's meat is another's poison, and that no amount of "book larnin'" will avail if the student does not put his knowledge to an actual test in the market.

It is surprising how an acquaintance with subjects relative to the stock market, but seemingly having no bearing upon Tape Reading, will lead to opportunities or aid in making deductions. It is therefore best to study everything possible about the subject. And so when asked what books will best supplement these Studies, I should say: Read everything you can get hold of. If you find but a single idea in a publication it is well worth the time and money spent in procuring and studying it. **Necessity of Study**

Wall Street is crowded with men who are there in the hope of making money, but who cannot be persuaded to look at the proposition from a practical business standpoint. Least of all will they study it, for this means long hours of hard work, and Mr. Speculator is laziness personified. Frequently

I have met those who pin their faith to some one point, such as the volumes up or down, and call it Tape Reading. Others, unconsciously trading on mechanical indications, pretend to be reading the tape. Then there is a class of people who read the tape with their tongues, calling off each transaction, a certain accent on the higher or lower quotations indicating whether they are bullish or bearish. These and others in their class are merely operating on the superficial. If they would spend the same five or six hours a day (which they now practically waste) in close study of the *business* of speculation, the result in dollars would be more gratifying at the end of the year. As it is, the majority of them are now losing money.

It is a source of satisfaction, however, that these Studies which, I believe, are the first practical articles ever written on the subject of Tape Reading, have stirred the minds of many people to the possibilities in the line

**Scientific
Speculation**

of scientific speculation. Evidence of this is found in the numerous communications received in response to my recent invitation; many of them from traders situated in remote localities.

In the main, the writers, who are now carrying on long distance operations for the big swings are desirous of testing their ability as Tape Readers.

No doubt those who have written represent but a small percentage of the number who are thus inclined.

To all such persons I would say: Before you can make a success of Tape Reading you must acquire a broad fundamental knowledge of the market. A professional singer who was recently called upon to advise a young aspirant said: "One must become a 'personality'—that is, an intelligence developed by the study of many things besides music." It is not enough to know a few of the underlying principles; one must have a *deep* understanding.

To be sure it is possible for a person to take a number of the "tricks of the trade" herein mentioned and trade successfully on these alone. Even one idea which forms part of the whole subject may be worked and elaborated upon until it becomes a method in itself. There are endless possibilities in this direction., and after all it matters little *how* the money is extracted from the market, so long as it is done legitimately.

**Endless Possibilities**

But real Tape Reading takes everything into account—every little character which appears on the tape plays its part in forming one of the endless series of "moving pictures." In many years' study of the tape, I do not remember having seen two of these "pictures" which were duplicates. One can realize from this how impossible it would be to formulate a simple set of rules to fit every case or even the majority of them, as each day's session produces hundreds of situations, which, so far as memory serves, are never repeated.

The subject of Tape Reading is therefore practically inexhaustible, which makes it all the more interesting to the man who has acquired the "study habit."

**Practical Study**

Having fortified himself with the necessary fundamental knowledge, the student of Tape Reading should thoroughly digest these Studies and any others which may be obtainable in future. It is not enough to go over and over a lesson as a school boy does, driving the facts into his head by monotonous repetition; tapes must be procured and the various indications matched up with what has been studied. And even after one believes he understands, he will presently learn that, to quote the words of a certain song, "You don't know how much you know until you know how little you know." One of my teachers in another line of study used to make me go over a thing three or four times after I *thought* I knew it, just to make sure that I did.

I should say that it is almost impossible for one who has never before traded from the tape to go into a broker's office, start right in and operate successfully. In the first place, there are the abbreviations and all the little characters and their meanings to be learned. It is not enough to know the abbreviations of the principal stocks; it is necessary to know *everything* that appears on the tape, so that nothing will be overlooked. Otherwise the operator will be like a person who attempts to read classic literature without knowing words of more than four letters.

It is a common impression in the Street that anyone who has the price can buy a seat on the Stock Exchange and at once begin making money as a floor trader. But as has already been shown in THE TICKER, floor trading is a business that one has to learn, and it usually takes months and years to become accustomed to the physical and nervous strain and learn the ropes.

**Floor Trading**

Frequent requests are made for the name of someone who will teach the Art of Tape Reading. I do not know of anyone able to read the tape with profit who is willing to become an instructor. The reason is very simple. Profits from the tape far exceed anything that might be earned in tuition fees.

In addition to the large operators and floor traders who use Tape Reading in their daily work, there are a number of New York Stock Exchange members who never go on the floor, but spend the session at the ticker in their respective offices. Experience has taught them that they can produce larger profits by this method, else they would not follow it. The majority of them trade in 500-share lots and up and their business forms an important share of the daily volume.

**Intuitive Tape Reading**

A number of so-called semi-professionals operate on what may be termed intuitive tape reading. They have no well defined code of rules and probably could not explain clearly just how they do it, but they "get the money" and that is the best proof of the pudding.

The existence of even a comparatively small body of successful Tape Readers is evidence that money making by this means is an accomplished fact and should encourage others.

One of the greatest difficulties which the novice has to overcome is known by the slangy but expressive term, "cold feet." Too many people start and dabble a little without going far enough to determine whether or not they can make a go of it. And even those who get pretty well along in the subject will be scared to death at a string of losses and quit just when they should dig in harder.

For in addition to learning the art they must form a sort of trading character, which no amount of reverses can discourage nor turn back and which constantly strives to eliminate its own weak points such as fear, greed, anxiety, nervousness and the many other mental factors which go to make or unmake the profit column.

**A Trading Character**

Perhaps I have painted a difficult proposition. If so, the greater will be the reward of those who master it. As stated at the beginning, Tape Reading is hard work. There seems no good reason for altering that opinion.

If these Studies and those in the series which will follow are the means of adding a few more names to the list of successful speculators, whether they are Tape Readers or not, I shall feel compensated.

*The End*

# Two Good Days

**B**ELOW is a record of transactions made by me for account of a client, results having been obtained by following the methods suggested in my recent series on Tape Reading. The object is to show the possibilities along this line and to encourage the many who are now endeavoring to master the art.

It will be observed that out of fifteen transactions, figuring on the buying and selling prices alone, there were thirteen profits and only one loss. One transaction showed neither profit nor loss.

Seven trades were on the long side and eight on the short. The stock fluctuated between 166¾ and 170⅜ (3⅝ points) during these two sessions (November 22 and 23), and gave numerous trading opportunities.

All transactions were protected by a close stop, in some cases not more than ⅛ or ¼ from the original buying or selling price. These stop orders were not always put on the floor for the reason that in such active trading, stops could be changed or cancelled more quickly when they were carried in the head and executed "at the market" when the price hit the required figure.

Table Showing Two Days' Trades

| | | | Bought | Sold | Loss | Profit |
|---|---|---|---|---|---|---|
| 200 | Reading | long | 167½ | 168¼ | | ¾ |
| 200 | " | short | 167¼ | 168⅜ | | 1⅛ |
| 200 | " | long | 167¼ | 168¾ | | 1½ |
| 200 | " | short | 169⅝ | 169¾ | | ⅛ |
| 200 | " | short | 169 | 169½ | | ½ |
| 200 | " | short | 169⅛ | 170 | | ⅞ |
| 100 | " | short | 169⅝ | 170 | | ⅜ |
| 200 | " | short | 168⅛ | 169⅞ | | 1¾ |
| 200 | " | long | 168 | 168 | | even |
| 200 | " | long | 168¼ | 168¾ | | ½ |
| 100 | " | short | 168 | 169¼ | | 1¼ |
| 100 | " | short | 168⅛ | 169¼ | | 1⅛ |
| 200 | " | long | 168⅛ | 168½ | | ⅜ |
| 200 | " | long | 168¼ | 169 | | ¾ |
| 200 | " | short | 169¼ | 168⅜ | ⅞ | |
| 2700 | | | | | ⅞ | 11 |
| Commission | | | | | 3⅜ | |
| Tax (about) | | | | | ¼ | |
| | | | | | | 4½ |
| Net profits, in points | | | | | | 6½ |

Milton Keynes UK
Ingram Content Group UK Ltd.
UKHW022143080923
428346UK00005B/186